Insights from African American Interpretation

Insights from African American Interpretation

Mitzi J. Smith

Fortress Press
Minneapolis

INSIGHTS FROM AFRICAN AMERICAN INTERPRETATION

Cover image: Brooklyn Bridge/Andres Garcia Martin/Thinkstock & Cruz de
Tejeda/emregologlu/Thinkstock
Cover design: Alisha Lofgren

Print ISBN: 978-1-5064-0017-4
eBook ISBN: 978-1-5064-0113-3

The paper used in this publication meets the minimum requirements of American
National Standard for Information Sciences — Permanence of Paper for Printed
Library Materials, ANSI Z329.48-1984.

Manufactured in the U.S.A.

This book was produced using Pressbooks.com, and PDF rendering was done by
PrinceXML.

Contents

Series Foreword

"What does this mean?"

That is, perhaps, the most-asked question with regard to the Bible. What does this verse mean? What does this story mean? What does this psalm or letter or prophecy or promise or commandment mean?

The question can arise from a simple desire for information, or the concern may be one of context or relevance: What *did* this mean to its original audience? What *does* it mean for us today?

Someone has said that understanding the Bible is difficult not because meaning is hard to find but because it is so abundant. The problem for interpreters is not *too little meaning* but *too much*. The question becomes, which of all the possible meanings is to be preferred?

But is that really a problem? And, if so, is it not a lovely one?

This abundance of meaning became especially clear in the last decades of the twentieth century when the field of biblical studies embraced dozens of new methods and approaches that had not previously been used or appreciated within the guild. In many ways, biblical studies became more exciting than ever before.

But, yes, the task of understanding the Bible could be daunting. Bible teachers, clergy and lay, who had struggled through college or seminary to learn "the historical-critical method" were suddenly confronted with novel strategies drawn from many other fields of inquiry: sociology, psychology, world religions, cultural anthropology, communication theory, modern literary criticism, and so forth. Then came the avalanche of interpretive approaches grounded in particular philosophical or ideological perspectives: feminism, postmodernism, liberation theology, postcolonialism, queer theology, and on and on.

For the open minded, the yield was an embarrassment of riches. We now understand the Bible in so many different ways: its historical witness, its theological message, its emotional impact, its sociocultural significance, its literary artistry, its capacity for rhetorical engagement, and so on.

At this point in time, we probably understand the Bible better than any who have gone before us. The Bible may challenge us more deeply than it challenged our forebears—and, yet, we have discovered that the Bible also seems to invite us (perhaps to *dare* us) to challenge it back. Many insights into the meaning of Scripture have come from people doing exactly that.

This *Insights* series from Fortress Press presents brief volumes that describe the different ways in which modern scholars approach the Bible, with emphasis on what we have learned from each of these approaches. These are not boring books on esoteric methodology. Some attention, of course, needs to be paid to presumptions and procedures, but the emphasis in each book is on the practical "pay-off" that a given approach has for students and teachers of the Bible. The authors discuss the most important insights they have gained from their approaches and they provide examples of how those insights play out when working with specific biblical texts in actual real-world circumstances.

Each volume discusses:

- how a particular method, approach, or strategy was first developed and how its application has changed over time;

- what current questions arise from its use;

- what enduring insights it has produced; and

- what questions remain for future scholarship.

Some volumes feature traditional approaches while others focus on new and experimental ones. You will definitely learn things in every book. Your current understanding of "what the Bible means" will be increased. And if you find that the "type of meaning" gained from a particular approach is not what interests you, perhaps you will nevertheless be grateful for the brief tour of a topic that fascinates some of your peers. The books are intentionally brief: they allow us to sample strategies and perspectives, to look down various avenues and see where they lead. They facilitate informed decisions regarding where we might want to go next.

I trust that we are now past the point of arguing over which approach to Scripture is the correct one. Such squabbles were part of the growth pains associated with the guild's aforementioned discovery that meaning is abundant, not so much elusive as ubiquitous.

Those of us who were professors during the late twentieth century sometimes helped our students deal with the methodological confusion by reminding them of the old Indian fable about six blind men and an elephant. In one well-known version of that tale, each of the blind men encounters an elephant and decides "what an elephant is like" based on his singular experience: one feels the trunk and says an elephant is like a hose; another, the tusk and says it is like a spear; another, the ear and says it is like a fan; another, the side and says it is like a wall; another, the leg and says it is like a tree; another, the tail and says it is like a rope. Later, when the men compare notes, each of them insists that he alone understands what an elephant is like: his comrades are totally mistaken.

So, we told our students in the 1990s, each biblical approach or method yields some valid insight into "the meaning of the Bible" (or into "the mystery of divine revelation" or into "what God wants to say to us"). But we would be wise to listen to those whose experience with the Bible is different from ours.

The Insights series is born of humility: its very existence is testimony to our commitment that we need to compare notes about the Bible with openness to each other's diverse perspectives. But, beyond that, I would hope that these volumes might also lead us to admit the limits of our perception. We now see, as the apostle Paul puts it, "in a mirror dimly" (1 Cor 13:12).

Many, including myself, who study the Bible believe it is the word of God, meaning it is a source of divine revelation. For this reason alone, the meaning of the Bible is abundant and ubiquitous.

We probably understand the Bible here and now better than any other people in history, and this triumph has brought us to the realization of how little we can understand, now or ever. But, insights? Yes. Those we can claim. Our experiences, our knowledge, and our perspectives do have authenticity and from them we have at least gained some *insights* into the meaning of Scripture. Time to compare notes!

MARK ALLAN POWELL

1

Introducing African American
Interpretation

[Y]ou know, people tells you, don't talk politics, but the air you breathe is polluted air, it's political polluted air. The air you breathe is politics. So you have to be involved.

—Fannie Lou Hamer (1917–1977)[1]

The Politics of Interpretation

Biblical interpretation is political. And as African Americans well know, biblical interpretation has always been political. The political is inherently hierarchal, in that some people are considered as superior to others who are constructed as inferior and subordinated. The political is concerned with the control of and access to resources, knowledge, and power. The power attributed to the Bible is profoundly demonstrated in the 2010 American postapocalyptic film *The Book of Eli*. Denzel Washington's character, Eli, has in his possession a powerful, sought-after book that his adversary and local warlord, Carnegie (played by Gary Oldman), will stop at nothing to obtain, read, and possess. Carnegie thinks that by reading the book he can control the world. In the first

---

1. Fannie Lou Hamer, "It's in Your Hands," in *Black Women in White America: A Documentary History*, ed. Gerda Lerner (New York: Vintage, 1972), 613.

1

fighting scene between Carnegie and his crew and Eli, Carnegie says the following to Eli: "I need that book. I mean I want it and if you make me choose, I'll kill you. . . . I grew up with it. I know its power." In a later scene, when one of his men states that he will assemble a crew and go after the book, Carnegie shouts these words: "It's not a fuckin' book. It's a weapon! A weapon aimed right at the hearts of the weak and the desperate. It will give us control of them. If we want to rule more than one small town we have to have it. People will come from all over. They'll do exactly what I tell them if the words are from the book. It's happened before and it'll happen again." The book in question turns out to be the Bible, which Eli has committed to memory. Carnegie, and the audience, does not realize that Eli is blind, thus the book is in Braille, a language only Eli can read. Thus, when Carnegie captures the book, he cannot read it. The connection between biblical literacy, interpretative agency, and the exercise of hegemonic power over the most vulnerable is indeed nothing new. The relationship is organic and fundamental to the history of European colonization, enslavement, and racialization of peoples of color or nonwhites.

Many consider the Bible as without doubt the number-one-selling and most widely distributed book in the world. And yet a number of sources are sounding the alarm about a twenty-first-century crisis of biblical illiteracy; people are not reading the Bible.[2] Many Christians rely on pastors, Sunday/Sabbath school teachers, television evangelists, and scholarly and nonscholarly books and commentaries to read and interpret the Bible for them. African American Christians are not exempt from this crisis of biblical illiteracy. And yet some of our African ancestors risked limb and life to be able to access and interpret the biblical text for themselves, to know for themselves the Jesus or God of the Book.

What happens when you tell a people that God is in a book or that God speaks through a book and then deny those same people access to that very book? This is precisely the story of enslaved Africans in America. It is no wonder that some African Americans became people of the Book and interpreters of the Book. Historically, biblical literacy could possibly give African Americans access to civil rights, as well as to the "word of God." The politics of race in the mid-twentieth cen-

---

2. Bill Stetzer, "Biblical Illiteracy by the Numbers Part 1: The Challenge," *Christianity Today* (October 17, 2014), http://www.christianitytoday.com/edstetzer/2014/october/biblical-illiteracy-by-the-numbers.html; Stetzer, "The Epidemic of Biblical Illiteracy in Our Churches," *Christianity Today* (July 6, 2015), http://www.christianitytoday.com/edstetzer/2015/july/epidemic-of-bible-illiteracy-in-our-churches.html.

tury, during the civil rights era, necessitated that some black Americans learn to recite large portions of Scripture in order to vote. Black people's inability to read and write, due to years of prohibition against black literacy and the paucity of schools available to black people after emancipation, effectively allowed former enslavers to prevent blacks from registering to vote. But some black people bypassed literacy, memorizing entire passages of the Bible and/or of the U.S. Constitution.[3] As black people gained physical and intellectual access to the Scriptures, reading and memorizing them, their interpretations informed their own politics and political involvement. Like many other civil rights activists, Fannie Lou Hamer understood her political activism as imitation of Jesus's pattern of acting out of concern for others rather than focusing on building million-dollar buildings while the people in the community starve.[4] Hamer insisted that if Christ walked the earth in 1968 people would brand him "a radical, a militant, and . . . as 'red' [i.e., a communist]."[5] Reading the Bible has always been and continues to be both a political and a theological undertaking. The theological is political, and the political is very often supported by contextual theological constructions.

This book discusses how African Americans have participated in the political, academic, and theological enterprise of biblical interpretation. It is not a comprehensive treatment of African American biblical interpretation or of the contributions of African American scholars to the field of biblical studies. Rather, I attempt to discuss and provide examples of many of the significant contributions and/or insights that African American and womanist (as its sister/companion hermeneutical perspective) biblical interpreters have made to the discipline. This chapter offers an introduction to some historical precursors, basic presuppositions, and general hermeneutical objectives of African American biblical interpretation from the perspective of one African American/womanist biblical scholar.

African American biblical scholars follow in the footsteps of

3. Septima Poinsette Clark, *Echo in My Soul* (New York: Dutton, 1962), 136–37. An illiterate woman and resident of Johns Island (one of the South Carolina Gullah islands), according to educator and civil rights worker Septima Clark, had memorized an entire section of the Constitution in order to register to vote; when she went to register she feigned reading the Constitution while actually reciting from memory.
4. Rosetta Ross, *Witnessing and Testifying: Black Women, Religion, and Civil Rights* (Minneapolis: Fortress Press, 2003), 114. See also Elice E. Rogers, "Afritics from Margin to Center: Theorizing the Politics of African American Women as Political Leaders," *Journal of Black Studies* 35, no. 6 (2005): 701–14.
5. Marcia Y. Riggs, *Can I Get a Witness? Prophetic Religious Voices of African American Women: An Anthology* (Maryknoll, NY: Orbis, 1997), 179.

Africans, enslaved and free, and their hermeneutical encounters with the Bible as oral performance and written text. The first black interpreters were introduced to the Bible sermonically and/or catechetically. Ideological and contextual interpretations of the Bible were performed before enslaved audiences and impressed and imposed upon their memories in order to justify their enslavement.

There appears to be some evidence that Africana peoples (those persons of African ancestry who reside either on the continent of Africa or in the diaspora beyond the continent) may have been reading, questioning, and interpreting the Scriptures or biblical texts before the Middle Passage that forcefully exiled them to strange lands and before the establishment of Christianity as an institutionalized religion distinct from Judaism. In the first century CE, according to the New Testament book the Acts of the Apostles, Africans from Ethiopia (the Ethiopian eunuch, a high official in the royal court of the Candace, the Queen of Ethiopia, 8:26–40) and from Alexandria in Egypt (a Jewish man named Apollos, 18:24—19:1; 1 Cor 1:10–17) possessed, read, studied, and interpreted Israel's sacred texts found in the Hebrew Bible (or in the Greek translation, known as the Septuagint [LXX]). In possession of a copy of Israel's Scriptures, the Ethiopian eunuch read, questioned, and invited the evangelist Philip to dialogue with him about the Isaiah scroll so as to understand better the text's contemporary relevance for him. The royal Ethiopian eunuch returned home a baptized believer in Jesus as the Jewish Messiah. We might presume that he shared his new understanding of the Scriptures with the Candace and others on the continent. The Egyptian Jewish man Apollos eloquently preached the gospel in both the Jewish and African Diasporas.

Apollos was not the only person of African descent preaching in the Jewish and African Diasporas. In the late nineteenth century the Antioch Baptist Church located in the American South eponymously and implicitly bore witness to other ancient interpreters of African descent belonging to the assembly of believers in Antioch of Syria (Acts 13:1). The church, originally called the Anti-Yoke Baptist Church, was renamed in 1890. Formerly enslaved Africans constructed the original structure that is currently displayed at the only slave museum in America, The Whitney Plantation Slave Museum in Baton Rouge, Louisiana, which I had the pleasure of visiting in the summer of 2015. The church's name acknowledges the Africans who prophesied and taught in the first century and whom the Holy Spirit instructed to lay hands on/anoint the apostles Paul and Barnabas for the work of ministry to which they were called. Those Africans ministering in Antioch were identified as Simeon called Niger and Lucius the Cyrene. Newly freed slaves in the American South interpreted those names to be of African descent. Thus, biblical interpretation by and/or among persons of African descent, focusing on the African presence, is not a novel phenomenon. Nor is a christocentric faith or hermeneutic among Africana peoples unique.

The history of Africans in the New World is marked by the capture and forced exile of Africans from their homeland. Black bodies were uprooted from land, language, culture, community, and family and transported into a distant geopolitical space where they would become collective racialized human property. This social uprooting was done in order to construct a nonhuman labor machine, stripped of all previous identity and agency, that could assist in European expansionism, constructing "new worlds" with the capital of and on the backs of enslaved black bodies. To assuage the captors' collective conscience and to rationalize the brutality of African enslavement, the colonists and/or religionists claimed to be conscripting the descendants of Ham and Cain, so-called black progenitors prescribed by God in sacred Christian texts as cursed and innately predestined to be the slaves of white men, the descendants of Japheth (Gen 9:18–27). The Christian Bible, understood as the literal, inerrant word of God, was said to have ordained some to be masters/enslavers and others to be enslaved. And so it was taught and preached to enslaved and free, young and old, religious and nonreligious. The story of enslaved Africans and the biblical stories of peoples conquering and being conquered in the name of God and gods are similar. To re-read both is to read stories of colonization, enslavement, hybridity, and decolonization. Thus, the interpretative history of enslaved and free African and African Americans in America can be understood as a history of decolonizing hermeneutics characterized by suspicion, rejection, and exposure of oppression as well as a quest for the re-membering or recovery of identity, self-worth, culture, language, community, and self-determination in a strange land.

The ultimate hermeneutical goal for enslaved Africans was, of course, freedom from bondage. In the interim the question they pondered was "How shall we sing Yahweh's song in a strange land?" This hermeneutical question was predicated upon the existential predicament of their enslavement. What relevance has Yahweh's song for the enslaved African in this foreign and hostile land? In what hermeneutical key shall they sing Yahweh's song?

Enslavers of African peoples intended that the Bible and racially biased interpretations of it should function as the mythical and psychological lock on enslaved black bodies, on their souls and minds. But many of the enslaved were suspicious of the Bible or the white man's interpretation of the Bible. They practiced what philosopher Paul Ricoeur later coined a "hermeneutics of suspicion." As Hebrew Bible Scholar Stephen Breck Reid notes, "long before any black pastor [or scholar of any race] heard [used or coined] the phrase, 'hermeneutics of suspicion,' black people used it."[6] Enslaved Africans were suspicious of the religionists of the book (and for not a few, the religion itself), the interpreters and interpretations of the book, and portions of the biblical text itself.

Some are familiar with the story of Nancy Ambrose, an illiterate former slave and the grandmother of the acclaimed African American theologian Howard Thurman. Unable to read the Bible for herself, Ambrose relied on young Howard to read for her. However, Ms. Ambrose prohibited her grandson from reading most Pauline texts to her; an exception was the reading of the Pauline love chapter, 1 Corinthians 13. Ms. Ambrose had experienced her fill of sermons centered on Pauline texts urging slaves to obey their masters. She rejected much of the Pauline canon and all interpretations that rendered slavery as God's chosen method for subjugating black people to white people, while elevating the latter.

Early African slaves and African American interpreters attempted to make the biblical text their own because they were convinced that God did indeed speak from, through, or in the text. Many of the enslaved were taught and believed that their only access to God, the God of the Christian religion, was through the biblical text to which they had been denied access. A hermeneutical deficit was imposed upon the enslaved, creating a hermeneutical conundrum and impasse for many. Enslavers, their designated preachers, and catechists taught the enslaved that their only access to God was through the Bible, as an early nineteenth-century Protestant Episcopal catechism stated: "Q: How do you know this [that God made all things including 'you']? A: God has told me so. Q: Where has God told you so? A: In his own book, called the Bible."[7] Many such catechetical questions concluded with the answer that "[God] has

6. Stephen Breck Reid, *Experience and Tradition: A Primer in Black Biblical Hermeneutics* (Nashville: Abingdon, 1990), 85.

7. Mitzi J. Smith, "U.S. Colonial Missions to African Slaves: Catechizing Black Souls, Traumatizing the Black *Psychē*," in *Teaching All Nations: Interrogating the Matthean Great Commission*, ed. Mitzi J. Smith and Lalitha Jayachitra (Minneapolis: Fortress Press, 2014), 57–88, at 68.

told me so in the Bible."[8] The very essence of God, including divine knowledge and salvation, was inextricably and organically connected with the Bible to which the enslaved were denied access.

The enslaved responded in various ways to the fact that they could neither possess the Book nor learn to read it. Many rejected the Christian religion, for valid reasons, unable to come to terms with their lived reality and the Christian God. Because enslavers and oppressive white men and women controlled access to the text, the gospel, and Christianity, some black people rejected Christianity and religion altogether. Former slave Henry Bibb wrote that thousands of slaves were "driven" "into infidelity" by preachers serving up a gospel that sanctioned slavery and commanded slave obedience to slavemasters. According to Bibb, enslaved Africans suffered unjustly, were friendless, and received protection of neither law (except "lynch law") nor gospel.[9] While some rejected the God and/or religion of the book as the God of white slave masters, others stealthily and with assistance risked limb and life to learn to read. And still others relied on personal revelations from the God who demonstrated no favoritism toward peoples based on skin color.

Those enslaved Africans in America who chose not to reject the Christian religion were convinced that if they could access the God who spoke through and in the text, they would hear something different. Such access had been denied them by prohibitions against teaching enslaved Africans to read and write. The literary trope of the talking book poignantly demonstrates the hermeneutical dilemma of enslaved Africans. When some illiterate slaves saw catechists and preachers stand before them with catechism or Bible open and read from them, the enslaved presumed that the book was talking to the reader. So, at the first stolen opportunity, the enslaved would press his or her ear to the open book. But his or her efforts were met with a deafening, disappointing silence; it was not a self-interpreting, talking book.[10] Former slave James Albert Ukawsaw Gronniosaw wrote the following account:

> [My master] used to read prayers in public to the ship's crew every Sabbath day; and when first I saw him read, I was never so surprised in my whole life as when I saw the book talk to my master; for I thought it did,

8. Ibid., 70.
9. Henry Bibb, "Narrative of the Life and Adventures of Henry Bibb, an American Slave, Written by Himself . . . (1849)," in Slave Narratives, ed. William L. Andrews and Henry Louis Gates Jr. (New York: Library of America, 2000), 425–566, at 446.
10. Allen Dwight Callahan, The Talking Book: African Americans and the Bible (New Haven: Yale University Press, 2006), 13.

as I observed him to look upon it, and move his lips.—I wished it would do so to me.—As soon as my master had done reading I follow'd him to the place where he put the book, being mightily delighted with it, and when nobody saw me, I open'd it and put my ear down close upon it, in great hope that it wou'd say something to me; but was very sorry and greatly disappointed when I found it would not speak, this thought immediately presented itself to me, that everybody and everything depis'd me because I was black.[11]

While the talking-book trope often refers to the Bible, I think the above quote refers to a catechism or an actual book of prayers. Catechisms written in rote question/answer format included select prayers and songs to reinforce servile behavior from the enslaved as supposedly sanctioned by God. The master of the ship on which Gronniosaw sailed would want to do everything in his power to control the mind and heart of the enslaved in order to avoid mutiny, and the prayers wrote specifically for the enslaved would serve his purpose well. B. M. Palmer's *Plain and Easy Catechism* contained a number of prayers, including this one: "Help me to be faithful to my owner's interest . . . may I never disappoint the trust that is placed in me, nor like the unjust steward, waste my master's goods."[12]

Former African slave Olaudah Equiano wrote a similar account about reading books generally: "I had often seen my master and Dick employed in reading; and I had a great curiosity to talk to the books, as I thought they did; and so to learned how all things had a beginning: for that purpose I have often taken up a book, and have talked to it, and then put my ears to it, when alone, in hopes it would answer me; and I have been very much concerned that I found it remained silent."[13] The above examples poignantly affirm on a very basic level that the biblical text is not self-interpreting, and that the degree of one's (il)literacy affects how and what one reads. Some enslaved Africans came to understand that in order for the Book (and books generally) to talk to them, like it talked to the slave master's preacher and to slave owners, they had to learn to read and to write for themselves. Some who

11. James Albert Ukawsaw Gronniosaw, "A Narrative of the Most Remarkable Particulars in the Life of James Albert Ukawsaw Gronniosaw, an African Prince, As related by Himself (1772)," in Andrews and Gates, eds., *Slave Narratives*, 1–34, at 11–12.
12. Rev. B. M. Palmer, *A Plain and Easy Catechism, Designed Chiefly for the Benefit of Coloured Persons, to Which Are Annexed Suitable Prayers and Hymns* (Charleston, SC: Observer Office Press, 1828), 32.
13. Olaudah Equiano, "The Interesting Narrative of the Life of Olaudah Equiano, or Gustavo Vassa, the African. Written by Himself (1789)" in Andrews and Gates, eds., *Slave Narratives*, 49–242, at 86.

learned to read did so by reading the Bible, which was often their greatest desire.

For some enslaved Africans who gained access to the Bible by learning to read (or learned to read by acquiring access to the Bible), their newly attained literacy confirmed their suspicion that it matters what one chooses to read, who reads, and how one reads. Many enslaved Africans did not need access to the biblical text, to the "talking book," to know to read against the grain of texts like "slaves, obey your masters." Those enslaved Africans knew that God created all human beings equally, despite what text the preacher "took" (selected it to sermonically expound upon). Some knew intuitively that God loved them and did not sanction their enslavement. Bibb wrote the following about a meeting he was given permission to attend on a neighboring plantation, where the owner was neither a "Deacon nor a professor of religion": "we had no Bible—no intelligent leader—but a conscience, prompted by our own reason, constrained us to worship God the Creator of all things."[14] Still other enslaved Africans could not reconcile the tragic and horrendous condition into which they were forced with the existence of a loving, all-powerful God; God had forsaken them.

Enslaved Africans struggled with and tried to make sense of their faith in God in the context of their oppression. Some things have not changed. African Americans continue to struggle with the issue of theodicy: How does one understand black suffering in light of one's faith in an all-powerful, all-knowing, always-present, loving, compassionate, and just God? In their song called "Dear God (I and II)," the contemporary neo-soul hip hop group The Roots headed by Questlove, ask a perennial question, "Why is the world ugly when you [God] created it in your image?" This question continually haunts black people and other oppressed peoples of faith in the world.

Reading for Freedom

Before being forced to endure (or die in) the Middle Passage as human cargo destined for the auction blocks of the New World, not a few Africans practiced African Traditional Religions (ATRs) or indigenous religions, as well as Catholicism, Islam, and Judaism. Thus, some enslaved Africans arrived in the New World as papists (Catholic), Muslims, and as Jews.[15] The Lemba people of Zimbabwe are a Jewish tribe

---

14. Bibb, "Narrative of the Life," 508.
15. Callahan, *The Talking Book*, 2; Equiano, "Interesting Narrative," 58.

of scientifically confirmed Semitic origin. It is claimed that the Lemba's Jewish ancestors fled the Holy Land about 2,500 years ago. It is possible that their Jewish ancestors settled in various places on the continent of Africa. Many Lemba in Zimbabwe are Christians and some are Muslims while maintaining their cultural roots in Judaism.[16] Whether the Africans forcefully brought to the New World were papists, Muslims, Jews, practitioners of ATRs, or a synthesis, they likely had inherited an African worldview that maintains the existence of a supreme God/Goddess who created the world and that all life, especially human life, is sacred.[17] Belief in a supreme being (sometimes called Asa, Olodumare, Oba, Shango, Chuku, and many other names) and the sacredness of life was counterintuitive to ideologies and biblical rationales concocted to support the forced exile and enslavement of Africans. Africans enslaved in America knew God as "the God of Liberty," "the God of justice," and "God of heaven."[18] Black freedom did not begin with the signing of the Emancipation Proclamation; Africans new freedom and God in Africa. The God of freedom was not born in the New World. God (and later Jesus) was known to be preexistent and prior to the enslavement of Africans.

Enslaved Africans and African American biblical interpreters and/or scholars have and continue to read the Bible for freedom—freedom from racist ideologies supporting their enslavement, from oppressive interpretations of the biblical text, and from hermeneutical constructions of a God and Jesus who despises black people. They read for freedom from spiritual, emotional/psychological, social, and physical bondage. Many enslaved Africans sang the Lord's song in the key of freedom, love, and justice, with a melody of hope and faith. For Henry Bibb, one could not be a "Bible Christian" and a slaveholder, which meant he interpreted the Scriptures differently from "slaveholding professors of religion" who saw no hypocrisy in being a professed Christian and enslaving human beings as property. Christianity must be practiced in accordance with the principles of humanity and justice.[19] Freedom for all humanity and love composed the overarching

---

16. Steve Vickers, "Lost Jewish Tribe 'Found in Zimbabwe'," BBC News, March 8, 2010. http://newsvote.bbc.co.uk/mpapps/pagetools/print/news.bbc.co.uk/2/hi/africa/8550614.stm?ad=1. Accessed February 2, 2017. My student, Shonagh Chimbira, informed me of the existence of the Lemba.

17. Equiano, "Interesting Narrative," 183; Bibb, "Narrative of the Life," 447–48.

18. Bibb, "Narrative of the Life," 483, 524; Equiano, "Interesting Narrative," 168, 187.

19. Bibb, "Narrative of the Life, 562, 563.

interpretive key for those enslaved Africans who accepted Christianity and the God of the biblical text.

Enslaved Africans and free(d) African Americans, in their attempt to make Christianity their own, engaged in a hermeneutical quest that could be understood in terms of continuity and discontinuity. They sought to understand and demonstrate the continuity between their intuitive conceptualization of a supreme creator God who loves all people, who did not create them for servitude or enslavement, and the God about whom the Scriptures testified. Early African American interpreters attempted to demonstrate the discontinuity between slave ideology, enslavement, and the biblical witness.

A major function of oppressive interpretations of the biblical text was their use to condone and rationalize the subordination, enslavement, and control of Africans in America. This rationalization included the erasure of the significant presence and contributions of persons of African origin from the biblical text. Those oppressive interpretations and reconstructions of the biblical text were aimed at the very identity of black peoples in America, to persuade them that the identity that their enslavers constructed for them was accurate because the Bible "told them so." In fact, enslavers attempted to inscribe in the very souls of black people through catechism schools the inferiority of the black race and the sanctity of their subordinate social position in relation to white people. African slaves were not only catechized to believe that they could only know God or Jesus through the Bible and the slave-master and/or preacher, but that only the latter had access to the book and its interpretation.[20] The enslaver and his surrogates had unfettered access to the ear and heart of God.

African American biblical interpretation makes use of a diversity of methodological tools, some of which were tools in the enslaver's hands. African American writer and activist Audre Lorde asserts, "the master's tools will never dismantle the master's house."[21] Black women and men must define and empower themselves and their communities. Lorde further states, "An old and primary tool of all oppressors" is "to keep the oppressed occupied with the master's concerns."[22] That some tools were also utilized by the enslavers does not preclude others using them in more liberating ways.[23] We can reappro-

20. Smith, "U.S. Colonial Missions."
21. Audre Lorde, *Sister Outsider* (Freedom, CA: Crossing, 1984), 112.
22. Ibid., 113.
23. Mitzi J. Smith, "Slavery in the Early Church," in *True to Our Native Land: An African American New*

priate some of the master's tools (e.g., the biblical text, biblical interpretation) and use them for liberation, for freedom.

(II)literacy, Revelation and Hermeneutical Agency

African American biblical interpretation affirms that the God of the Bible speaks to black people. The Bible and Eurocentric interpretations of it had become a primary means for constructing a rationale for enslaving, oppressing, and excluding black people. Thus, the experience of revelation, of God revealing God's self to black people despite their inability to read the Bible for themselves became central for black people's self-understanding and self-confidence. God's unmediated self-revelation remains a central aspect of African American biblical interpretation. Black people believe that God's revelation is not limited to white people; that God reveals God's self to people of color. And it is this truth that first and foremost legitimizes black people's authority to read and interpret the biblical text. God's self-revelation to black people and other people of color reaffirms their full humanity and hermeneutical agency or their right to read the biblical text through the lens or framework of and in dialogue with black people's humanness, loves, traditions, artifacts, concerns, joys, and struggles, past and present.

Gaining access to the God of the Bible was a chief concern for enslaved and free African Americans. While a few enslaved Africans related how they encountered a white master, a child, or some other slaves who taught them how to read, others like Nat Turner claimed to have received direct revelation from God. God's Spirit revealed to Turner the meaning of a text he had heard and committed to memory. Turner never learned to read, but he could decipher words in the Bible, having never learned, to his recollection, the alphabet.[24] Nat Turner mentions having attended meetings at which he heard someone quote (loosely) Matthew 6:33 (or Luke 12:47?): "Seek ye first the kingdom of Heaven and all these things shall be added unto you."[25] More than likely, in the original context in which it was introduced to Turner, it was being used to keep the slaves docile and looking for a reward in the

Testament Commentary, ed. Brian K. Blount, with Cain Hope Felder, Clarice J. Martin, and Emerson B. Powery (Minneapolis: Fortress Press, 2007), 11–22, at 19.

24. Nat Turner, "The Confessions of Nat Turner, the Leader of the Late Insurrection in Southampton, VA . . . (1831)," in Andrews and Gates, eds., *Slave Narratives*, 243–66, at 250.

25. Ibid., 251.

by and by. But that text resonated with Turner; he seemed to memorize it, consciously or unconsciously. He wrote:

> I reflected much on this passage, and prayed daily for light on this subject—As I was praying one day at my plough, the spirit spoke to me, saying, 'Seek ye the kingdom of Heaven and all things shall be added unto you.' *Question*—what do you mean by Spirit. *Ans.* The Spirit that spoke to the prophets in former days—and I was greatly astonished, and for two years prayed continually, whenever my duty would permit—and then again I had the same revelation, which fully confirmed me in the impression that I was ordained for some great purpose in the hands of the Almighty. Several years rolled round. . . . At this time I reverted in my mind to the remarks made of me in my childhood . . . that I had too much sense to be raised, and if I was, I would never be of any use to any one as a slave. Now finding I had arrived to man's estate, and was a slave, and these revelations being made known to me, I began to direct my attention to this great object, to fulfil the purpose for which, by this time, I felt assured I was intended.[26]

Interestingly, Turner structures his conversation with the Spirit and the Spirit's answer in the similar way that questions and answers are provided in catechisms. Many, especially during the Second Great Awakening, were taught to memorize answers to biblical questions presented them through catechisms (some written and published especially for slaves) and Sabbath school lessons. Also, significantly, Turner's reading or revelation did not encourage him to assume a passive and nonviolent approach to the injustices he and other enslaved Africans were experiencing in the present world. Instead, he was encouraged to physically "put his hand to the plough" and become an agent of change with regard to the unjust enslavement of Africans.

Other enslaved and freed Africans claimed to be the recipients of special divine revelation as well, and such revelations trumped the biblical text (or oppressive interpretations) and functioned as the interpretative framework for constructing a hermeneutic that favored the enslaved's predicament. Nineteenth-century African American preaching women Old Elizabeth and Zilpha Elaw announced and demonstrated how God revealed God's self to black women when white and black male clergy and parishioners rejected the possibility of such experience. Those black preaching women read their calls and revelatory experiences in tandem with or analogous to and drawing from the

---

26. Ibid.

apostle Paul's call narratives and other Pauline rhetoric and images. They were among the early female or proto-womanist (embodying a womanist ethic that values and prioritizes black women's experience and knowledge before the term was coined in the twentieth century) interpreters of biblical texts and black religious experience.[27] Zilpha Elaw's commission to preach (or interpret the Bible publicly) originated "not from mortal man, but from the voice of an invisible and heavenly personage sent from God."[28] God revealed to Zilpha Elaw that they did not have to have the tools—the literacy, mentoring, and training—that men had in order to "gird up thy loins like a man" and publicly interpret and preach the gospel to mixed audiences of women and men.[29] Just as white male experience is not universal for white women and men of color, black male experience is not universal for black women.

Undeniably Interested, Cultural, and Ideological

While all approaches to biblical interpretation are contextual and ideological, contemporary scholars tend to reserve such designations for minoritized interpretive approaches and not for the dominant, mainstream methods. African American biblical interpretation is an unapologetically, undeniably interested, ideological, culturally determined, contextual approach to reading biblical texts and contexts, as well as readings and readers of biblical texts and contexts. It is fair and correct to understand all interpretations and interpreters are culturally located. And all interpretive methods are ideological and subjective. Every interpretation is filtered through the interpreter or the reading subject engaged in the act of interpretation/translation. Every interpreter approaches the reading task, from beginning to end, with preconceived ideas and beliefs. The reader selects a text. A particular text may inspire or draw her in, but she *selects* the text out of her experiences, needs/desires, passions, traditions, and identity. Through her experiences, needs/desires, passions, traditions, and identity she chooses to engage some texts and to ignore other texts as part of the interpretive process. The selection process is culturally and/or contextually informed and has political consequences—consequences for how one lives and interacts with others, negotiates relationships of power,

27. See Mitzi J. Smith, "'Unbossed and Unbought': Zilpha Elaw and Old Elizabeth and a Political Discourse of Origins," *Black Theology* 9, no. 3 (2011): 287–311.
28. Ibid., 304.
29. Ibid., 305.

exercises or relinquishes agency, receives or distributes resources, validates or undermines authority. Readers engaged in African American biblical interpretation select texts based on the privileging of a particular cultural or ideological lens associated with their identity, traditions, and experiences. Such selectivity allows African American interpreters to critically address particular issues relevant to Africana women, men, children, and other marginalized groups.

A Legitimate Hermeneutical Lens

African American experience and traditions are presumed legitimate hermeneutical lenses, and do not merit marginalization. As New Testament scholar Brian Blount argues, "minority opinions may be entertained" but "they lack political legitimation and, therefore, power."[30] In fact, minority opinions are ignored or dismissed as illegitimate and/ or not scholarly and thus marginally engaged, if at all. African American biblical hermeneutics continue to challenge the exclusion of African American and other minoritized voices and their concerns in the academy, and in biblical studies more particularly, which is often considered and/or treated as the cornerstone of the academy and religious studies. Historical-critical methods portend to engage in objective exegesis and continue, if implicitly, to assert that to arrive at a plausible and legitimate interpretation of biblical texts, one must in some way give priority to Eurocentric voices and historical-critical methods. Yet, scholars who use historical-critical methods often disagree, even with hostility and indignation, as to how particular texts and contexts ought to be understood, despite their use of the same tools. Consequently, Eurocentric biblical scholars produce a plethora of diverse interpretations of one text. But those interpretations are usually considered more legitimate than those produced by minoritized scholars who refuse to prioritize that which is behind the text. African American biblical interpretation rejects this hierarchy of methods that prioritizes Eurocentric approaches.

As another biblical scholar, Vincent Wimbush, argues, our readings, the interpretations, knowledge, truths we produce are not "*misreadings*" in the hegemonic, white sense of the meaning; they are not foreign babble that often go unacknowledged.[31] African American biblical

---

30. Brian L. Blount, Cain Hope Felder, Clarice Martin, and Emerson Powery, "Introduction," in Blount, et al., eds., *True to Our Native Land*, 1–7, at 3.
31. Vincent L. Wimbush, ed., *MisReading America: Scriptures and Difference* (New York: Oxford University Press, 2013), 2–3.

interpretation or sacred knowledge production has been dismissed and called *racist* by white and nonwhite keepers of the Eurocentric canon. Fear overtakes the gatekeeper because his identity is wedded to and inextricably intertwined with a method or methods that strategically and intentionally bans overt appeals to the culture and concerns of the other. In a white-constructed world, Wimbush argues, "some among nonwhite communities have reconceptualized and embraced the association of being black or brown or . . . with some sort of 'lack,'" resulting in tragic *misreadings*.[32]

Relevance Is a Priority

While mainstream/malestream biblical interpreters attempt to convince readers that what is behind the biblical text, its history, and some hypothetical original authorial intent is more important than what's happening in front of the text, the interconnected realities of racism, sexism, classism, and other -isms are killing people of color and the poor.

African American biblical interpretation attempts to construct readings that are relevant to black communities and other oppressed peoples. It is about doing biblical interpretation that critically reflects and engages the lived experiences (struggles and achievements), culture, traditions, and epistemologies of African Americans. It takes seriously the mundane impact of (neo)colonization marked by systemic or structural racism, denial and violation of human and civil rights of people of color, and other interrelated oppressions. Africana biblical interpreters recognize the absence or dearth of interpretations that address issues relevant to black communities, including racism, classism, poverty, and social justice. In 1976, Howard Thurman wrote in his book *Jesus and the Disinherited*: "Many and varied are the interpretations dealing with the teachings and the life of Jesus of Nazareth. But few of these interpretations deal with what the teachings and the life of Jesus have to say to those who stand, at a moment in human history, with their backs against the wall."[33]

Civil rights worker Septima Clark (1898–1987) understood the Scriptures as mandating the destruction of systemic oppression, stating the following: "If we really are to contribute to the 'deliverance of the captives' it is necessary to do something to redeem the system which

---

32. Ibid., 3.
33. Howard Thurman, *Jesus and the Disinherited* (Boston: Beacon, 1976), 11.

keeps them in captivity."[34] Clark, as well as her sisters in the struggle, Fannie Lou Hamer and Ella Baker (1903–1986), articulated the need
for change and the uplift of oppressed blacks (and whites) in moral
terms; they employed the biblical Christ and biblical texts to motivate
toward political involvement. These civil rights icons used the Bible
to propel their own continued involvement in the struggle despite
setbacks, drawbacks, and immobility. Christ became the paradigmatic
example to motivate people to do right by other people and to serve
the people according to their needs. Clark described her participation
in the Highlander Folk School (a social-justice training facility where
civil rights strategies were mapped out among black and white atten-
dees) in accordance with how she interpreted the life of Christ:

> I do not like to be described as a negro leader fighting for the integration
> of the schools, the churches, the transportation facilities, the political par-
> ties, or whatnot. I don't consider myself a fighter. I'd prefer to be looked
> on as a worker, a woman who loves her fellow man, white and negro alike,
> and yellow, red, and brown, and is striving with her every energy, work-
> ing—not fighting—in the true spirit of fellowship to lift him to a higher
> level of attainment and appreciation and enjoyment of life. I hope that I
> have—surely I wish to possess and I do strive to attain—something of the
> spirit of the lowly and glorious young Man of Galilee, *who as I read him
> and understand him* and worship him, saw no color or racial lines but loved
> with a consuming devotional all of the children of God and knew them all
> as his brothers.[35]

Religion professor Rosetta Ross states that "Clark's interpretation of
Scripture coincides with the legacy in Black Christian traditions that
evaluates the Bible based on its relevance for daily life."[36]

African American biblical scholars can prioritize cultural and contextual relevance *and* use historical-critical methods. Like other biblical scholars, trained in the academy, they address historical contexts
(including issues of authorship, social relationships, and life situation),
ancient sources and literary forms, revisions or editorial changes to
such forms and sources, variations in ancient manuscript traditions,
and other concerns. But that which lies behind the text does not determine the questions to be asked of the text; a search for the ancient
historical context does not drive the hermeneutical task. Significant
questions propelling African American biblical interpretation include

34. Ross, *Witnessing and Testifying*, 82.
35. Clark, *Echo in my Soul*, 132 (emphasis mine).
36. Ross, *Witnessing and Testifying*, 78.

the following: How is the biblical text relevant to the predicaments in which black people and other peoples of color find themselves? How do we speak of God, Jesus, and/or the Holy Spirit in ways that are meaningful, life giving, freeing, and prophetic in light of the colonized past and (neo)colonized present? What can Jesus, God, the Spirit, and biblical texts mean and say to the most oppressed and vulnerable in our communities and beyond? How have black women and men read the biblical text in the past and how can such readings inform the present? How have African Americans allowed themselves, their lives, to be read and/or challenged by texts? How might we understand Scripture when it contradicts God/Goddess's revelation to the reader and the reader's experience? What are readers to do with Scriptures that encourage or reinscribe stereotypes, violence and oppressions (e.g., heterosexism, racism, classism, sexism, ageism, or bias against physically challenged persons)? African American biblical interpretation functions to provide relevant, freedom-engendering interpretations as sites of consciousness raising and political activism.

African American biblical interpretation calls attention to the ways in which traditional, Eurocentric biblical interpretation has and continues to construct oppressive interpretations and theologies, wittingly and unwittingly. Mainstream biblical interpretation continues to reflect and perpetuate the privileged concerns, ideas, and positions of cis-gendered white males to the exclusion of those that derive from communities of color and other minoritized groups.[37] As an academic endeavor, African American biblical interpretation claims or reserves the right to read sacred texts critically; it refuses to accept Eurocentric interpretations as normative for all people, as universal. In fact, to do so has proven deleterious and/or fatal to black health and life.

Affirms the Sacredness of Black Lives

African American biblical interpretation affirms the sacredness of black life and freedom in contexts where such are daily contested; black lives matter! It matters when people of color and poor people "cannot breathe." It affirms that it is important to recognize the impact of interlocking oppressions on the lives of black women and their children; say her name! African American biblical interpretation affirms that poor women and children, as well as non-cisgendered people of

---

37. Cisgendered is the opposite of transgendered. With cisgendered people, their gender corresponds to their assigned sex, which is the vast majority of people.

color are often the most vulnerable in our society. It reaffirms the sacredness of African Americans (and other people of color) and their communities. They, too, are (a) God-inspired readers or interpreters of the Bible or Scripture and other sacred cultural texts and contexts; (b) sources and creators of sacred knowledge; and (c) fully capable of defining their relationship to Scripture and the God about whom it testifies. African Americans assert that they are neither empty nor inferior slates, but that they have and continue to make valuable and necessary contributions to the process of biblical interpretation and to the field of biblical studies.

Historically, African American biblical interpreters have engaged in a sacred hermeneutical quest to demonstrate and confirm the spiritually intuited disjuncture between racist ideological interpretations of the sacred texts and a supreme God/Goddess who shows no favoritism.[38] Black people as sacred interpreters have rejected the so-called biblical justification for the enslavement and subordination of black peoples to white peoples. They have challenged the metanarrative that God predetermined and ordained that black peoples were inherently inferior to white peoples and were consequently created to serve white peoples, as descendants of Ham and Japheth, respectively. While exercising their interpretive agency, African Americans have (re)constructed and articulated their own identity as full human beings in relation to God and their fellow human beings; named and defined themselves for themselves; and attempted to empower black communities and churches with a gospel message relevant to their needs and to the times in which they live, struggle to survive, and thrive.

Chapters 2 and 3 of this book describe some significant developments of African American and womanist biblical interpretation in the twentieth and twenty-first centuries, respectively. I discuss the various interdisciplinary methodologies used by African American biblical scholars to produce interpretive works that are of relevance to Africana peoples. Both chapters explore the interdisciplinary character and emphases of African American biblical interpretation, seminal publications, hermeneutical innovations, and ways in which it has and continues to expand in terms of its use of and/or engagement with diverse critical theories, methodologies, voices, traditions, artifacts,

---

38. The term *Goddess* signifies, emphasizes, and celebrates the feminine traits of the Divine. According to the Priestly account of creation, God made both male and female, humankind, in the image or likeness of Elohim (Gen 1:26–27). See my blog post, "God is a Black Woman and She is Divine," March 11, 2011. http://womanistntprof.blogspot.com/2011/03/god-is-a-black-woman-and-she-is-divine.html.

and (con)texts. I discuss and demonstrate some important African American and womanist biblical interpretation contributions to the field of biblical studies.

African American biblical interpreters have challenged and/or attempted to rectify oppressive Eurocentric interpretations that for centuries used the Bible to preach a gospel of inferiority and oppression. They have recovered the black presence and significance in the biblical texts; addressed the dilemma of exclusion and invisibility faced by blacks entering academic study of the Bible; insisted upon the black women's unique experience and interpretative perspectives; and expanded the interpretative canon beyond biblical texts to include cultural artifacts and traditions. African American biblical interpretation privileges the experiences, voices, stories, traditions, and artifacts of Africana peoples. From those resources, black scholars approach biblical texts to construct perspectives or vantage points from which to critically read texts, readers, readings/interpretations, interpreters, and contexts.

Chapters 4 and 5 consist of African American readings of biblical texts—one is a reading of a New Testament text and the other from the Hebrew Bible, respectively. In both readings I create a dialogue between the ancient (con)text and historical and contemporary African American traditions and experiences. In chapter 4, titled "Slavery, Torture, Systemic Oppression, and Kingdom Rhetoric: An African American Reading of Matthew 25:1–13," I read the parable about the ten virgins as a part of a trilogy of slave parables that reinscribe stereotypes about master/slave relationships. My African American lens privileges black people's experience with systemic structures of oppression, constructing dialogue between the ancient text of the parable and African American lived realities, engaging postcolonial and other theories. In chapter 5, titled "Dis-membering, Sexual Violence, and Confinement: A Womanist Intersectional Reading of the Story of the Levite's Secondary Wife (Judges 19)," I develop a theory of dis-membering as a process of social death, affected by gender, class, and race and characterized by denial of access to the same protections that are afforded to certain privileged members of the dominant society. I argue that the mutilation and death of the Levite's secondary wife was the final stage of her dis-memberment.

Acknowledgments

I am thankful to Insights series editor Dr. Mark Allan Powell for believing in my work enough to invite me to write this book and for his invaluable feedback that definitely helped to improve upon its final form. I, of course, take full responsibility for the final manuscript. I dedicate this text to my first biblical studies professors at Howard University School of Divinity, Drs. Cain Hope Felder, Michael W. Newheart, and the late and truly missed Gene Rice (1925–2016), who first taught me how to do biblical interpretation. This text is also dedicated to my former Harvard dissertation advisor, colleague, and friend, Dr. François Bovon (1938–2013), who encouraged me and affirmed the significance of intuition for doing biblical interpretation. Most of all, I dedicate this work to my mother, Flora Carson Ophelia Smith (1927–2009) who was my first and most dearly beloved teacher and mentor.

2

Twentieth-Century Foundations

The first professionally or academically trained African American biblical scholars emerged in the twentieth century and laid the foundation for African American biblical interpretation as an approach or method for doing biblical interpretation.[1] Most, if not all, of those scholars sought to do biblical interpretation that would both satisfy the needs and desires of their own souls and would be relevant to and resonate with the collective heart and mind of black churches and communities. Those first black biblical scholars had been shaped by and were situated within the elite academic professional guild, whose majority membership consists of mature white men. Many black biblical scholars had been greatly affected by, grew up in, participated in, and continued to contribute to the ongoing life of the black church as preachers, pastors, and Sunday school teachers. Sometimes the expectations of the professional guild conflicted with the needs of black communities and churches. Black scholars themselves, as members of both guild and church, found it difficult, if not impossible, to satisfy the demands of the academic guild, including the institutions that employed them, and simultaneously produce scholarship accessible and relevant to black churches and communities. African American New Testament

---

1. According to Michael Joseph Brown (*Blackening the Bible: The Aims of African American Biblical Scholarship* [Harrisburg, PA: Trinity, 2004], 19), Leon Wright was the first African American to earn a doctorate in New Testament studies, from Howard University, in 1945.

scholar Michael Joseph Brown has argued, in his book *Blackening the Bible*, that the fruits of African American biblical interpretation have eluded the larger black community, including black churches.[2] Brown's observation is largely, but not completely, correct in my view. Twentieth-century attempts by African American biblical scholars to bridge the gap between their scholarship and the larger black church and community enjoyed some successes (for example, the publication of Afrocentric Bibles and the book *Just a Sister Away* by Renita Weems, the first black female Hebrew Bible scholar, have both enjoyed widespread acceptance in black churches and will be mentioned in greater detail below).[3]

This is not to say the relationship between black biblical scholars and black churches and communities has been without its own problems. Sometimes African American biblical scholarship has been outright rejected by conservative black leadership and laypeoples who, among other things, are not accustomed to hearing their own voices (as New Testament scholar William H. Myers has expressed it); they are comfortable with the familiar and they are familiar with conservative Eurocentric biblical interpretation and the white Jesus. Much of the black church has been convinced that intellectualism and spirituality make strange bedfellows and should be divorced from one another in order for the latter to thrive. Still, African American biblical scholars have struggled to write for the black community, to be public scholars/theologians, despite having been trained to write for the academy and to replicate a Eurocentric hermeneutic. As Myers notes, most often it has not been Eurocentric academic or seminary training that prepared the African American student to articulate "an African American hermeneutic in their ministerial context or academic position."[4] African American scholars and students have had to articulate the needs and draw upon the traditions, culture, and experiences of the black community, starting with the way in which the Bible and biblical interpretation has been used against black people. African American biblical scholar Cain Hope Felder has argued that "The Eurocentric mind-set has tended to prescribe the rhythms, specify the harmonies,

---

2. Ibid., 23.
3. Cain Hope Felder, ed., *The Original African Heritage Study Bible*, King James Version (Iowa Falls, IA: World Bible Publishers, 1993); Renita Weems, *Just a Sister Away: A Womanist Vision of Women's Relationships in the Bible* (San Diego: LuraMedia/Philadelphia: Innisfree, 1988) (see also n. 58, below).
4. William H. Myers, "The Hermeneutical Dilemma of the African American Biblical Student," in Cain Hope Felder, ed., *Stony the Road We Trod: African American Biblical Interpretation* (Minneapolis: Fortress Press, 1991), 40–56, at 56.

and determine the key signatures for everyone's scholarship."[5] Furthermore, Eurocentric or "mainstream" biblical scholarship functioned under the pretense that it was neither culturally contextual nor ideological.[6] Nevertheless, as stated in chapter 1, African American biblical interpreters and interpretation have always utilized a hermeneutics of suspicion—suspicion about the Eurocentric enterprise of biblical interpretation that whitewashed the biblical text and privileged the voices and concerns of the "winners" and/or authors of the text; about the majority white interpreters of the text; and about the biblical text itself and its context. African American biblical interpreters, engaged in the politics of interpretation, attempted to recover their own interpretive agency, voice, and freedom as well as the agency, voices, and freedom of the marginalized black communities for whom the Bible is both a sacred and authoritative text.

Recovery, Significance, and Relevance of the African Presence

Traditionally, for Eurocentric biblical scholarship, the African presence in the biblical text was irrelevant or only significant for the purposes of demonstrating the subordination of black peoples to white peoples and the superiority of the latter over the former. In the twentieth century, black biblical scholars attempted to counteract the whitewashing of the Bible by recovering the African presence and its significance. But these pioneering biblical scholars would also subversively address attacks on the black presence and identity in America; they would attempt to read the Bible for those who needed to hear a word from God amidst the daily assaults on their person, identity, and communities. Freedom was never free; the price of admission was calculated, cruel, and supported by racist ideologies undergirded by Eurocentric biblical interpretation.

When the first black biblical scholars entered the academic guild, about 120 years, or approximately five generations, had passed since the signing of the Emancipation Proclamation in 1865. Less than one hundred years after emancipation, the United States passed the Civil Rights Bills of 1957 (establishing a civil rights commission and civil

---

5. Cain Hope Felder, "Introduction," in Felder, ed., *Stony the Road We Trod*, 1–14, at 7.
6. Many books on biblical interpretation include separate chapters on cultural and ideological studies (with a marginal mention of African American biblical interpretation), as if mainstream biblical interpretation is neither cultural nor ideological. Also, some texts do not even include the works of African American biblical scholars in their brief discussions of African American biblical interpretation and womanist criticism. See, for example, W. Randolph Tate, *Biblical Interpretation: An Integrative Approach* (Peabody, MA: Hendrickson, 1997).

rights division in the Justice Department) and 1964 (prohibiting discrimination on the basis of sex as well as race in hiring, promoting, and firing), then the Voting Rights Bill of 1965 (eliminating literary tests for black citizens). Between the emancipation of millions of African slaves and the passing of civil and voting rights legislation, American blacks had experienced legalized and de facto segregation and discrimination, lynching and disenfranchisement, and systemic racism. Most early black biblical scholars lived through the period of "blacks-only" restrooms and drinking fountains, race riots, in the shadows of the "strange fruit" of lynched black bodies that dangled from "poplar trees," whites-only or segregated public spaces like schools, pools, and restaurants, desegregation and white backlash, the civil rights movement, and the black power movement. This string of unrelenting blows aimed at the black body and collective community in America wounded the bodies, minds, and spirits of black people, their sense of self-worth and self-identity. Often, oppressive interpretations of biblical texts were used to deliver the ideological blows of racism. It was in this context that early African American biblical scholars focused their efforts on recovering the black presence and its significance within the sacred history and narrative of the biblical text. Their project was one of correcting the ways that Eurocentric biblical interpreters and interpretations misconstrued or misrepresented the biblical traditions, giving the impression that the God of the Bible favored white people, and that the Bible was the white man's book and the foundational text of his religion.

It was important for black people to know that they were not an inferior afterthought, more associated with sin than with God's initial creative act; it mattered who (re)told the story. Charles B. Copher (1913–2003), one of the earliest professionally trained biblical scholars, argued that biblical history, geography, archaeology, and other affiliated studies should acknowledge the presence of "Black persons of all classes from Pharaohs to slaves,"[7] male and female. Copher demonstrated that African peoples are a significant organic part of the history and narrative of the Bible, from the creation story to the book of Revelation. He cautioned readers, however, that the African experience in the Bible is provided from the "perspective of Hebrew Israelite-Judahite-Jewish" writers, except where authorship could be attributed

---

7. Charles B. Copher, *Black Biblical Studies: An Anthology of Charles B. Copher* (Chicago: Black Light Fellowship, 1993), 13. See also Frank M. Snowden Jr., *Blacks in Antiquity: Ethiopians in the Greco-Roman Experience* (Cambridge, MA: Harvard University Press, 1970).

to African persons.[8] Thus, he essentially argued for a hermeneutics of suspicion concerning the ethnocentric Jewish character and perspective of the text. Nevertheless, the Bible had a place in the lives of African peoples from before its canonical inception up to the present, Copher argued. He called for black peoples to become leading commentators and interpreters of the biblical text. Other topics that should be of great significance to biblical scholarship, Copher asserted, are how African peoples understood, interpreted, and employed the biblical text, as well as African authorship of biblical texts. For example, Moses, who some believed had authored the Pentateuch, was born and raised in Egypt, which is in Africa.[9] Indeed, Copher asserted, "No Africa, no biblical content."[10] In his 1995 essay in *The Recovery of Black Presence* (RBP), Old Testament scholar Randall C. Bailey uses Pentateuchal source criticism and argues that the earlier Jahwist (J) and Elohist (E) traditions present Moses as an Egyptian while the later Priestly source (P) re-presents him as an Israelite man.[11]

Integral to the quest for black presence, agency, and identity in the Bible is the need for relevance to the current plight of black peoples. As Copher argued, for biblical interpretation to be relevant for black seminarians, it must be done from a black and not just a white perspective. It must relate the Scriptures to black people's contemporary lives so that they resonate as a living word that dwells among us.[12] The recovery of the black presence is about demonstrating the Bible's relevance to black people beyond the supposed mandate for slaves to obey masters. Slavemasters or enslavers and later proponents of the inferiority of black people as a race clearly believed and propagated the idea that God sided with the white man. James Cone, the father of black theology and mentor to many early black biblical scholars, argued in the early 1970s that God sides with the oppressed, and the Bible is "God's Word to those who are oppressed and humiliated in this world."[13] Cone read the exodus story as parallel with the African American experience of

---

8. Charles B. Copher, "The Bible and the African Experience: The Biblical Period," *Journal of the Inter-denominational Theological Center* [*JITC*] 13 (1988): 57–79, at 62. See also Gene Rice, "The African Roots of the Prophet Zephaniah," *Journal of Religious Thought* 36, no. 1 (Spring-Summer, 1979): 21–31.
9. Copher, "The Bible and the African Experience," 60–61.
10. Ibid.
11. Randall C. Bailey, "'Is That Any Name for a Nice Hebrew Boy?' Exodus 2:1-10: The De-Africanization of an Israelite Hero," in *The Recovery of Black Presence: An Interdisciplinary Exploration*, ed. Randall C. Bailey and Jacquelyn Grant (Nashville: Abingdon, 1995), 25–36.
12. Copher, *Black Biblical Studies*, 15.
13. James H. Cone, *God of the Oppressed* (Maryknoll, NY: Orbis, 1997), 9. Originally published in 1975 by Seabury.

slavery and emancipation. African American biblical scholars, through a recovery of the black presence, would subsequently demonstrate that God had never forsaken black folks. Black theology, initially a response to the black power movement, challenged black biblical scholars to avert their gaze from what the text meant so that they might focus on the meaning of the biblical text for the contemporary black community.[14]

Further, New Testament scholar Brian Blount challenged readers to recognize how potential meanings, not just a single meaning, can be negotiated with the text, particularly since the reader's interpersonal context has an impact on their reading of the biblical text.[15] In fact, at the end of the twentieth century, Blount would be the first African American biblical scholar to publish a monograph or book in which he interpreted a biblical book (Mark's Gospel) through the lens of African American black church experience.[16] The ability to read the Bible in ways that are relevant for black communities helps free black people from oppressive interpretations of texts that are dismissive of black culture, traditions, history (as American or African), and lived experiences. As New Testament scholar Obery Hendricks asserts, biblical interpretation is setting the oppressed free, making new readings and truths from old things, unapologetically asking relevant questions and challenging interpretations void of representation.[17]

Like Cone, Cain Hope Felder uses the Bible as a tool for liberation, albeit for him an "indispensable tool for . . . sociopolitical and economic, as well as spiritual" freedom.[18] In Felder's first book, *Troubling Biblical Waters* (TBW), he expands our knowledge of the significance of Egypt and Ethiopia by analyzing both biblical and extrabiblical sources. He also explores racial themes in the Bible. In addition to addressing issues of race, class, gender (addressing the sexism in the black church), and family (demonstrating that the Bible does not present the nuclear family as the norm; that a fictive kinship model includes the hurt and needy as family; and global peacemaking), Felder examines

---

14. See James H. Cone, *Black Theology and Black Power* (New York: Harper & Row, 1969); and Thomas Hoyt Jr., "Biblical Interpreters and Black Theology," in *Black Theology: A Documentary History, vol. 2: 1980-1992*, ed. Gayraud S. Wilmore and James H. Cone (Maryknoll, NY: Orbis, 1996), 196–209.

15. Brian K. Blount, *Cultural Interpretation: Reorienting New Testament Criticism* (Minneapolis: Fortress Press, 1995).

16. Brian K. Blount, *Go Preach! Mark's Kingdom Message and the Black Church Today* (Maryknoll, NY: Orbis, 1998).

17. Obery Hendricks, "Guerrilla Exegesis: A Post-Modern Proposal for Insurgent African American Biblical Interpretation," *JITC* 22 (1994): 92–109.

18. Cain Hope Felder, *Troubling Biblical Waters: Race, Class, Family* (Maryknoll, NY: Orbis, 1989), xiv.

the biblical mandate for social justice as a challenge to New Testament scholars who claim the absence of such a directive. Felder, like other early black biblical scholars, critically engages the biblical text in order to set the record straight about interpretations or ideas about the Bible that have had a harmful or oppressive impact upon the historical and contemporary socioeconomic situation of black people. He wishes to "provide sorely needed correctives for reading the Bible in relation to ancient Africa and Black people today."[19] Like Copher, Felder seeks to "illuminate the Black story within The Story, so the ancient record of God's Word takes on new meaning for the Black Church today."[20]

Out of a communal space of dialogue among black biblical scholars, female and male, emerged the first seminal text dedicated to the subject of African American biblical interpretation. The 1991 publication of *Stony the Road We Trod* (SRT), edited by Felder, marked the arrival of "a new phase in the tradition of black biblical scholars," as African American biblical scholarship was increasingly growing into a mature "tree near the dense forest of Eurocentric biblical exegesis and interpretation."[21] The Bible remained the central lens for reading the black story, and from the reader's engagement with the biblical texts the questions that should be raised emerge and the right answers are affirmed.[22] This latter understanding of the preeminence of the text reflects the black biblical scholar's Eurocentric professional training.[23]

The early quest for the African presence in the biblical texts also sought to understand its function. In his SRT essay "Beyond Identification: The Use of Africans in Old Testament Poetry and Narratives," Bailey analyzes the *significance* of the African presence to determine what it reveals about Israel's perception of Africans *and* how such Israelite perceptions illuminate the objective of the Hebrew Bible writers. How do Africans, as perceived and characterized, function in the narratives? Bailey finds, for example, that references to Egypt and Cush in the poetic sections of the prophetic, psalmic, and wisdom literatures function as ideals against which to judge or compare with Israel and Yahweh. The materials that Bailey examines "show that Israel held African nations and individuals in very high regard."[24] In his reading of Jere-

19. Ibid., xi.
20. Ibid.
21. Felder, "Introduction," 1.
22. Ibid., 30.
23. See Michael Gorman, *Elements of Biblical Exegesis: A Basic Guide for Students and Ministers* (Peabody, MA: Hendrickson, 2005).
24. Randall C. Bailey, "Beyond Identification: The Use of Africans in Old Testament Poetry and Narratives," in Felder, ed., *Stony the Road We Trod*, 165–84, at 178 and 183.

miah 13:23, Bailey offers a new translation rendering the text "Would the Cushite change his skin, or the leopard his spots?" rather than "Can the Cushite change. . . ." He argues that both the Cushite and the leopard have found that being accepting of and comfortable in their own skin is advantageous: "rulers of territories who are respected by and awesome to their neighbors."[25] In Jeremiah 13:23, the Cushites function as a standard by which Israel should assess themselves.[26] In a 1996 essay entitled "They Shall Become as White as Snow: When Bad Is Turned into Good,"[27] Bailey challenges translations (which are also interpretations) that reflect contemporary racist ideologies; ideologies of race function on the level of translation. He deconstructs the translations of Isaiah 1:18, particularly the verse that reads: "Though your sins be as scarlet, they shall be white as snow." He argues that "though" is translated from the Hebrew verb *'im*, which is normally rendered as "if" and in fact is translated as "if" at Isaiah 1:20. Scholars prefer to see the text in question as a blessing rather than a curse, but Bailey, using historical and literary criticism, argues it is a curse in the context of a judgment text. Bailey examines other instances of the verb "turning white" or to cause to turn white. In those instances, to turn something white constitutes a curse or a negative action. At Isaiah 1:18, Bailey argues, it is no different. Ideals of white as a symbol of normality have an impact on contemporary translations of biblical texts, and this tendency can be seen in translations of Isaiah 1:18 as well. Bailey is also addressing the intersectionality of race and religion in his challenge to translations of Isaiah 1:18 where "becoming white" is viewed as a blessing. He summons readers "to bring to consciousness the ways in which oppressive ideologies function in our translation/interpretation options."[28]

Biblical scholar Lloyd A. Lewis, in his SRT essay "An African American Appraisal of the Philemon-Paul-Onesimus Triangle," reads the language in Philemon together with Galatians, using its familial language as the interpretative key. Lewis considers Philemon within the framework of Pauline theology and ecclesiology, rather than Paul's chronology. Black readers no longer need understand the book of Philemon as only containing hateful words supporting slavery; it can be read as good news abolishing hierarchical social distinctions. Lewis's reading

---

25. Ibid., 176–77.
26. Ibid., 177.
27. Randall C. Bailey, "'They Shall Become as White as Snow': When Bad Is Turned into Good," *Semeia* 76 (1996): 99–113.
28. Ibid., 109.

of Philemon emphasizes the inclusion of all believers as children of God.[29]

The early focus on the black presence in the Bible also included examinations of female characters, usually by male scholars who outnumbered the first black female biblical scholars (Renita Weems and Clarice Martin). The first scholar to publish a book-length African American interpretation of the Hagar story was African American theologian Delores Williams. Her seminal text *Sisters in the Wilderness* offers a womanist theological perspective reading the Hagar (an Egyptian slave) story through the lens of black women's history of surrogacy, particularly as enslaved persons.[30] African American biblical scholar John Waters examines the social and ethnic identity of Hagar in SRT. He argues that, contrary to traditional Eurocentric biblical scholarship, Hagar was *not* a slave; Hagar was Egyptian, North African, and a free person. Waters arrives at this conclusion based on an analysis of the ancient sources that scholars argue may have been used to construct the narratives of the Pentateuch in their final form. Specifically, Waters examines the J (Jahwist) and E (Elohist) sources that contain distinct versions of the Sarah-Hagar Genesis narratives. For example, Waters analyzes the power dynamics between Hagar and Sarah and the agency Hagar demonstrates in obtaining an Egyptian wife for Ishmael. Waters asserts that Hagar was not enslaved by Abraham and Sarah in the same way that the Hebrews were enslaved to Egypt.[31] It appears that Hagar demonstrated freedoms and agency that the Hebrews could not exercise, including her flight from Sarai, unpursued, into the wilderness where she encountered and named Yahweh (Gen 16: 4–14, the Jahwist's version).

As the above examples demonstrate, Afrocentric approaches to biblical interpretation have served to combat the negative and oppressive impact of Eurocentric biblical interpretation that ignores, debases, and/or erases the black presence and significance from the biblical history and narrative. In addition to the silence about and/or obliteration of the presence and significance of African peoples in biblical history and texts, interpreters actively constructed readings that supported the racist ideologies about peoples of African descent, as noted in chapter 1. Twentieth-century African American biblical scholars,

29. Lloyd Lewis, "An African American Appraisal of the Philemon–Paul–Onesimus Triangle," in Felder, ed., *Stony the Road We Trod*, 232–46.
30. Delores Williams, *Sisters in the Wilderness: The Challenge of Womanist God-Talk* (Maryknoll, NY: Orbis, 1998 [1993]).
31. John W Waters, "Who Was Hagar?," in Felder, ed., *Stony the Road We Trod*, 187–205.

like ordinary black readers before them, also hermeneutically refuted the so-called curse of Ham interpretation of Genesis 9:18–27, which argued that black peoples, as descendants of Ham, were cursed and subordinated to white persons as descendants of Japheth.[32]

Only when it served to support the racialized subordination of black peoples did most Eurocentric biblical interpretation indicate the significance of the African presence in the Bible. Felder argues that racialized biblical interpretations based on racist ideologies about the inherent inferiority of one race to another amounts to *sacralization* (the process of making secular ideas sacred by interpreting biblical texts to support racist ideologies).[33] Some early interpreters understood Cain, as well as Ham and Canaan, and their descendants, which includes the modern black race, as cursed by God.[34] Such racialized and racist interpretations persist and continue to have an impact on individual theological understandings. In this twenty-first century, I had a conversation with an African American male, who is also a secondary-school educator, who insists that black people today are cursed, as stated in the Bible! African American biblical scholarship that addresses the African presence and its function in the Bible continues to be a relevant and necessary corrective, especially given the continual gap between church, community, and academy.

With the 1995 publication of RBP (four years after STR), edited by Randall Bailey and Jacquelyn Grant (a womanist theologian), African American biblical scholars continued to focus on the retrieval and reconstruction of the African presence and its significance in the biblical narratives. But African American biblical scholarship also went beyond its focus on the black presence in the Bible, expanded its interpretative approaches, and even attempted to decenter the biblical text. New Testament scholar Boykin Sanders's essay uses form, source, and canonical criticism, together with social anthropology (the works of Bruce Malina and Jerome H. Neyrey), arguing that Luke's characterization of Simon of Cyrene, an African *and* a non-Jewish man compelled to carry Jesus's cross, was of primary significance to the unfolding narrative; Sanders also argued that the story was likely historical.[35] A few

---

32. Felder, "Race, Racism, and the Biblical Narratives," in Felder, ed., *Stony the Road We Trod*, 129–35. See Gene Rice, "The Curse That Never Was (Genesis 9:18–27)," *Journal of Religious Thought* 29 (1972): 5–27.

33. Felder, "Race, Racism, and the Biblical Narrative," 134.

34. Charles B. Copher, "The Black Presence in the Old Testament," in Felder, ed., *Stony the Road We Trod*, 147–49. A pre-Adamite view argues that God created blacks or Negroes prior to Adam and from them Cain found his wife and became the progenitor of black peoples. A so-called New Hamite view erases the black presence from the Old Testament.

years before this, Brian Blount explored the strategic rhetorical and theological function of the Simon narratives in the Synoptic Gospels. He argued that Simon as an outsider functions in the representative role of a disciple who takes up his cross and follows Jesus. Luke's Simon demonstrates an inclusivity imitative of the Romans. Both Simon's identity and function demonstrate Luke's idea of discipleship that transcends or transgresses ethnographical borders.[36]

Another popular narrative among African American biblical scholars is the story of the Ethiopian eunuch in Acts 8:26–40. Several scholars have attempted to demonstrate its function in Luke's narrative. In an essay based on her doctoral dissertation, New Testament scholar Clarice Martin challenges Eurocentric scholarship's biased reading and description of the eunuch as a Jew and not an African. Martin argues that the eunuch functions in the narrative as a fulfillment of the spreading of the gospel to the "ends of the earth," as foretold in Acts 1:8c.[37]

In the twentieth century, scholars began reading culture and artifacts, including black people's interpretive production and/or representation of biblical or religious knowledge in fiction. For these scholars, the biblical text is not the primary text for biblical studies; it is decentered. For instance, Abraham Smith, a New Testament scholar, deviates from the above scholars and their use of historical-critical methods; his primary text is a novel written by African American author Toni Morrison. Smith uses literary criticism to read Morrison's use of biblical texts, characters, and names. He attempts to determine how the blues and the Bible function in Morrison's novel *Song of Solomon*, which might be the problem of adapting traditional values uncritically into contemporary contexts. Smith concludes that Morrison uses the Bible to warn about applying it and its labels in ways that are not relevant or applicable to life and real experiences.[38]

While Smith focuses on the tradition of African American fiction, William H. Myers constructs a contemporary version of the call narrative as an African American cultural tradition/artifact. Myers col-

---

35. Boykin Sanders, "In Search of a Face for Simon the Cyrene," in Bailey and Grant, eds., *Recovery of Black Presence*, 51–64.

36. Brian Blount, "A Socio-Rhetorical Analysis of Simon of Cyrene," *Semeia* 63 (1993): 171–98.

37. Clarice J. Martin, "A Chamberlain's Journey and the Challenge of Interpretation for Liberation," *Semeia* 47 (1989): 105–35; Martin, "The Function of Acts 8:26–40 within the Narrative Structure of the Book of Acts: The Significance of the Eunuch's Provenance for Acts 1:8c," PhD diss., Duke University, 1985.

38. Abraham Smith, "Toni Morrison's Song of Solomon: the Blues and the Bible," in Bailey and Grant, eds., *Recovery of the Black Presence*, 107–15.

lects and analyzes African American call narratives, both female and male, in his classic volumes, *The Irresistible Urge to Preach: A Collection of African American Call Stories* and *God's Yes Was Louder than My No: Rethinking the African American Call to Ministry*.[39] The former text was based on his PhD dissertation. In chapter 11 of the latter text, Myers discusses the continuities and discontinuities between the African American call narratives, biblical call stories, and similar narratives arising out of the African religious experience. Myers found continuity between African Americans' use of the call narrative to legitimize their claims to be God's instruments. He argues for an association with the "prior theological and cultural traditions"; these are the call stories of Judeo-Christian biblical tradition (e.g., Ezekiel's call), the emphasis on the "inner call" in American Protestantism, and the Shaman divine call to leadership and conversion stories within African Traditional Religion.[40] Myers's project constructs and collects a cultural artifact from African American experience, focusing on contemporary black identity and presence and its roots in the biblical tradition and beyond.

African American biblical scholars also hermeneutically challenged visual art, either in the biblical text or that (re)presented the Jesus of the biblical text, by producing versions of the Bible that reflected the African presence in its artwork and front matter. The visually, hermeneutically whitewashed Bible had now been aesthetically darkened or Africanized in response to the de-Africanization and whitening of the biblical text. If the visual imagery inserted into the biblical text could be Europeanized, it could certainly be Africanized. Thus, the publication of *The Original African Heritage Study Bible* (1993), edited by Cain Hope Felder, and the American Bible Society's *African American Jubilee Edition* of the Bible (1999) should be understood as subversive interpretive acts that visibly challenged whitewashed biblical texts.[41] African American theologian and art historian Sheila Winborne asserts that Paul Tillich became "the first western Christian theologian to construct a full theology of art." Winborne further states that "Tillich argued that [the silent language of the visual arts] can communicate theological and spiritual messages as powerfully and at times more power-

39. William H. Myers, *The Irresistible Urge to Preach: A Collection of African American Call Stories* (Atlanta: Aaron, 1992); Myers, *God's Yes Was Louder than My No: Rethinking the African American Call to Ministry* (Grand Rapids: Eerdmans/Trenton, NY: African Word, 1994).

40. Myers, *God's Yes*, 195–214.

41. Cain Hope Felder, ed., *Holy Bible: The African American Jubilee Edition*, Contemporary English Version (Philadelphia: American Bible Society, 1999); Felder, ed., *Original African Heritage Study Bible*. The latter remains in print and popular among African American Christians.

fully than words ... [and] can communicate concepts more clearly than words."[42] African American biblical scholars recognized the power of the white Christ that adorned black churches and other public spaces, homes, and some Bibles. They knew and experienced the deleterious psychological, social, and cultural impact of the whitewashed visual imagery in the biblical text that connected everything sacred and pure with everything white, even Jesus. If Jesus was white, then God must value and favor whiteness above all things black, since Jesus was God's only begotten son and also one with his Father, according to John's Gospel. The absence of black or African images in the sacred biblical text, together with the perpetuation of a widespread cultural narrative that subordinated black (and brown) peoples to white persons of European descent, reinforced the cultural narrative of race and class hierarchy. As Winborne argues, "[o]ne of the most powerful ways colonial ideologies about who are defined as *chosen* and *Other* have been communicated is through created images of Jesus rendered as racially white, with these representations marketed as the most 'true' or legitimate images of Jesus as Christ."[43] Africans and African Americans who embraced Christianity, a christocentric religion, were haunted by the white Christ, who reminded them of their supposed inferiority before God and the white race. The creation of the *African Heritage Study Bible* hermeneutically, through words and visual art, demonstrated that the Bible is not the white man's book, but it is inherently multicultural.

Early black biblical interpreters who focused on the black presence and its function in the biblical text and the use of biblical texts by black peoples were already interdisciplinary in their approach to biblical studies, as they brought together the disciplines of African/African American studies (including the study of African American literature and other cultural artifacts and traditions), archaeology and geography, and biblical studies. Looking back into the twentieth century and discussing the role of archaeology among early African American biblical interpretation (while also issuing a challenge for twentieth-first century scholars), Old Testament scholar and archaeologist Theodore Burgh discusses how black biblical scholars such as Copher, Felder, Bailey, Weems, and others have approached black biblical interpretation in an interdisciplinary way by, for example, using archaeology in

---

42. Sheila F. Winborne, "Images of Jesus in Advancing the Great Commission," *Teaching All Nations: Interrogating the Matthean Great Commission*, ed. Mitzi J. Smith and Lalitha Jayachitra (Minneapolis: Fortress Press, 2014): 159–73, at 165.
43. Ibid., 160.

their recovery of the black presence and challenging Eurocentric biblical scholarship's separation of Egypt from Africa.[44] Early black biblical interpreters expanded their interdisciplinary approach using archaeology and geography (a significant element of archaeology). African American biblical interpretation has enjoyed a fruitful relationship with Near Eastern archaeology, making connections between the biblical text and archaeological findings. Burgh argues that it is important to view the biblical text as both Scripture and an ancient artifact. Early models for interdisciplinarity include archaeology to discuss issues of chronology, geography, etymology and development of ancient cultures. In TBW, Felder uses an interdisciplinary approach to bring clarity to the ambiguity surrounding the location of Cush/Ethiopia in relationship to the Queen of Sheba. Bailey, in his SRT essay, demonstrates the significance of geography to challenge both the omission of Cush, Put, and Cyrene as nations of Africa and Eurocentric scholarship that removes Egypt from Africa by arguing for a clear boundary between sub-Saharan Africa and Egypt. Weems considers both geography, as well as ancient Near Eastern culture and artifacts, in her 1988 reading of Martha and Mary.[45] All these scholars direct our attention to Africa rather than away from Africa.

Black Identity, Self-Worth, and Biblical Interpretation

Intimately linked with the quest for the recovery of black presence and significance or relevance in the biblical text are attempts to remember, construct, and affirm black self- and communal identity and self-worth, as well as black experience. African Americans have and continue to live in the context of an oppressive racialized, gendered, and elitist society that has used and continues to use the Scriptures to diminish the value of black lives. Yet the Scriptures, as William Myers states, "have played [and continue to fulfill] an important role in helping African Americans to survive and maintain a healthy identity and hope."[46]

We see this valuing and affirmation of black identity and experience in Stephen Breck Reid's formative text *Experience and Tradition: A Primer in Black Biblical Hermeneutics.*[47] Reid argues that black biblical interpretation begins with black experience, which is not monolithic, and is

---

44. Theodore W. Burgh, "Black Biblical Interpretation and Near Eastern Archaeology," *Biblical Theology* 4, no. 2 (2006): 138–50.
45. Ibid., 139–45.
46. Myers, "Hermeneutical Dilemma," 45.

organized around black identity. For him, black identity begins with the black experience of slavery.[48] I think what Reid means by "black identity" is black identity in America, an identity imposed upon Africans in practice and by law through the creation of a racialized, socially constructed ("apartheid") system of stratification that subordinated, categorized and enslaved human beings primarily based on physiognomy (certain physical characteristics like hair texture, skin color, and full lips). Of course, the identity of African blacks connected with their homelands on the continent of Africa, which they knew before the Middle Passage, predated their experience as enslaved Africans in the "New World."

Reid argues that a black biblical hermeneutics challenges popular political theology and its attribution of power in the dominant group and the divestiture of power from the poor and minorities. As a quest for identity, black biblical theology interprets black experience and the biblical text, holding black culture and tradition in one hand and the Bible in the other. For Reid, three movements constitute black biblical hermeneutics as a method: "a critical reading of the text; the recovery of black interpretation of the text, and the application of the text to the life experience of the black community."[49] In the first movement Reid considers the sociohistorical context of the text but becomes critically aware of inappropriate power relationships within it; this movement is an act of *conscientization*, which reveals the deceptions at the foundation of oppressive ideologies.[50] In other words, the text and its context can be problematic and implicated in the construction and reinscription of oppression and oppressive structures.

Reid's second movement, the recovery of black interpretation, examines "the ways the black church and culture have interpreted biblical themes in order to reshape the power relationships of the believing community."[51] It is reading the text in the light of other stories, themes, and concerns of black experience. The third and final move is to extract a practical theology for the black church and community. Black biblical interpretation is christocentric; Christ, argues Reid, binds the black church together. But, of course, Reid is speaking of

---

47. Stephen Breck Reid, *Experience and Tradition: A Primer in Black Biblical Hermeneutics* (Nashville: Abingdon, 1990).
48. Ibid., 9.
49. Ibid.
50. The term *conscientization* was coined by Paulo Freire (*The Pedagogy of the Oppressed* [New York: Continuum, 1997], 49), referring to the process by which the oppressed become critically aware of their own oppression and that they must fight for their own liberation.
51. Reid, *Experience and Tradition*, 20.

black Christian churches; not all black churches and black religious folk are Christian. For example, many are Muslims who practice Islam. It is foundational to consider the unity of life holding together the cultural (intellectual) and material (socioeconomic realities, including the interplay of racism and capitalism) expressed in both Scripture and black life.

I find Reid's twentieth-century interpretation of Genesis 3–4 intriguing and relevant for twenty-first-century black lives and the ongoing conversation about violence in black communities located in large urban cities like Baltimore, Chicago, and Detroit. Reid examines the Adam and Eve and Cain and Abel stories in the historical context of the United Monarchy and the theological rationale for David and Solomon's ascensions to the throne despite not being the eldest sons; the eldest son is depicted as villain. Critical awareness is raised with regard to issues of deception/misinterpretation, self-hatred, partnership erosion, and partnership as miracle. Regarding the Cain and Abel story, Cain's fratricide (murder of his brother) is understood as a model for understanding so-called black-on-black crime. (Significantly, this is a phrase—a problematic one in my view—used increasingly in our present environment, by nonwhites and whites, in conversations about police brutality, profiling, and crime in poor minority neighborhoods. Nobody talks about white-on-white crime. Most people commit crimes against those in closest proximity to them and not because of the color of their skin, unless they are "hate crimes.") Reid notes that class conflict between shepherd and farmer is introduced into the story. Cain's birth order and occupation offended the royal storyteller. No reason is given for God's rejection of Cain's offering, and the question is asked of Cain, "if you do well, will you not be accepted?" (Gen 4:6). Reid argues that for the black community, the answer is "no." The victim, whose offering would be unsatisfactory regardless, is made the criminal. Cain is structurally blocked from succeeding or doing well because of his class and occupation. "Structurally, given the agenda of the Yahwist, there was no chance that Cain would succeed. He was an elder son in the court of the younger son. He was a farmer in the jurisdiction of shepherds."[52]

In his approach to doing black biblical hermeneutics, Reid locates the structural issues in the text *and* in contemporary black experience. In my view, it is almost impossible for readers to critique the biblical

---

52. Ibid., 40.

text if it is viewed as inextricably connected with the very essence of God. Felder has warned against treating the biblical text as if it is synonymous with God, urging readers to "liberate themselves from the popular tendency to deify the Bible.[53] Reid asserts that as a result of the capricious mistreatment of Cain, he murders his innocent brother Abel. "When you cannot effectively victimize those who structurally keep you out, then you victimize those close at hand."[54] In his application, Reid states that the response to the question "Am I my brother's keeper?" must yield a resounding "yes" from the black community. Because Cain lacked the power to coerce the structures that blocked him, he coerced one like himself. Subsequently, Cain is turned black after the crime to protect him from violence, whereas being black in America has tacitly sanctioned violence against black people.

Reid does what few African American biblical scholars had previously done: he critiques the characterization of God in the biblical text and/or the theological agenda embedded in or behind the construction of the text. Like other scholars before him, Reid starts with a critical analysis of the biblical text, but he exposes the structural oppression embedded in the text itself. The black church has never been a monolithic collective in terms of its view of the biblical text, never having assumed, wholesale, an uncritical stance toward it. While some members of black churches and communities still require and need to be assured or convinced that the Bible is not the white man's book, others need to know that it is acceptable to struggle with the God about which the Book testifies and the Bible itself, even while maintaining, or in order to sustain, a positive relationship with the Bible. Black biblical scholarship has shown black churches and communities that it is not inappropriate or taboo to question the biblical text, the God constructed by or in the biblical text, and/or the Eurocentric interpretative tradition. African American biblical interpretation continues to demonstrate the legitimacy of engaging black experience and addressing the needs of black communities in doing biblical studies.

History of Black Interpretation

It has been important for African American biblical scholars to understand how enslaved Africans and African Americans have interpreted the Bible in the past and how the Bible functioned in their commu-

---

53. Felder, *Troubling Biblical Waters*, 14.
54. Reid, *Experience and Tradition*, 41.

nities. According to Wimbush's examination of black interpretive history, initial reactions among African Americans included "rejection, suspicion, and awe"; they used the Bible for their own self-interest and self-affirmation in the context of slavery.[55] With the mass conversion of many African slaves to evangelical faith as taught by Methodist and Baptists, especially during the Second Great Awakening, black peoples increasingly learned to read the Bible (and the white readers of the Bible) for themselves and to read it selectively. Many enslaved Africans received the biblical text as oral text by way of sermons and/ or prayers, songs, and question/answer format in catechisms.[56] The enslaved retold biblical stories that reflected their own experiences. Wimbush argues that African Americans' use of the Bible in the eighteenth century, the classic period, is the basis upon which subsequent readings, to some degree, would be founded and evaluated.[57] African American biblical scholar David Shannon (1934–2008) argued for examining the sermons of black preachers to know their thoughts; he analyzed Paul Lawrence Dunbar's sermon in verse, "An Ante-bellum Sermon" to discover the hermeneutic principle embedded in the re-creation of an antebellum sermon.[58]

If It Wasn't for the Women: Race, Gender, and Class

As noted above, male biblical scholars like Felder, Reid, Shannon, and others have either addressed issues of gender and the black church or read female biblical characters like Hagar from a male perspective. Thus, African American biblical scholars have not neglected issues of gender or class even though primarily concerned with race. African American biblical scholars who have addressed issues of gender inequality within black communities have been motivated by a consciousness of the impact of gender oppression on the community as a whole, as well as on black women. In 1988, prior to the publication of TBW,STR and RBP Hebrew Bible scholar Renita Weems published her celebrated and widely acclaimed seminal book *Just a Sister Away: A Womanist Vision of Women's Relationships in the Bible.*[59] In her ground-

55. Vincent L. Wimbush, "The Bible and African Americans: An Outline of an Interpretative History," in Felder, ed., *Stony the Road We Trod*, 81–97, at 85.

56. See Mitzi J. Smith, "U.S. Colonial Missions to African Slaves: Catechizing Black Souls, Traumatizing the Black *Psychē*," in Smith and Jayachitra, eds., *Teaching All Nations*, 57–88.

57. Wimbush, "Bible and African Americans," 86–89.

58. David T. Shannon, "'An Ante-bellum Sermon': A Resource for an African American Hermeneutic," in Felder, ed., *Stony the Road We Trod*, 98–125, at 99.

59. Weems, *Just a Sister Away*. Weems's text has been revised and updated under the title *Just a Sister*

breaking (and perennially relevant) text, Weems, using a womanist perspective (a critical sister or companion hermeneutical approach to African American biblical interpretation; neither subordinate to nor subsumed under it), critically reads biblical stories involving relationships between two or more women (e.g., Sarai/Hagar; Mary/Martha; Naomi/Ruth; the women that follow Jesus). A womanist perspective privileges the experiences and traditions of African American women and acknowledges the impact of interlocking forms of oppression (race, gender, and class) upon the lives of black women. The term *womanist* was coined and defined by Alice Walker in her short story "Coming Apart" and later more broadly described in her 1983 book *In Our Mothers' Gardens*.[60] African American biblical interpretation and womanist biblical interpretation overlap and are sometimes fluid, but womanist interpreters (or black women scholars reading from a womanist perspective) argue that black men cannot speak for black women because they do not experience the triple intersection of oppression that results from being black, female, and disproportionately poor simultaneously, as do most black women.[61] Womanists hold in tension the privileging of black women's experiences and the quest for the wholeness and health of the entire black community, inclusive of black men and children. The stories, traditions, artifacts, and experiences of black men and women overlap and they diverge.

Having originated from an oral storytelling culture of the motherland (Africa), and having been thrust into a literate culture that denied them access to literacy, enslaved Africans in America and African Americans are part of a tradition that values and has an affinity for storytelling. In combining biblical interpretation and the African American storytelling tradition, Weems created interpretive reconstructions that uncover inclusive space for working out women's faith in relation to one another. Although Weems does not use the term *intersectionality* in her book, she does address the intersection or interconnectedness (the complexity) of race, gender, and class in, for example, the Sarai/Hagar narratives. For my master of divinity classmates and myself

---

Away: Understanding the Timeless Connection between Women of Today and Women in the Bible (New York: Warner/West Bloomfield, MI: Walk Worthy, 2005).

60. Alice Walker, "Coming Apart," in *Take Back the Night*, ed. Laura Lederer (New York: Bantam, 1979): 84–93; Walker, *In Our Mothers' Gardens: Womanist Prose* (San Diego: Harcourt Brace, 1983), ix.

61. For more information on womanist biblical interpretation, see Mitzi J. Smith, ed., *I Found God in Me: A Womanist Biblical Hermeneutics Reader* (Eugene, OR: Cascade, 2015); Wil Gafney, Womanist Midrash: A Reintroduction to the Women of the Torah and the Throne (Louisville: Westminster John Knox, 2017); and Nyasha Junior, *An Introduction to Womanist Biblical Interpretation* (Louisville: Westminster John Knox, 2015).

41

at Howard University School of Divinity, Weems provided a critical and relevant reading that reflected the experiences of flesh-and-blood African American women, which had not been previously available to us. African American women's experiences with the Bible could be characterized as ambivalent, given both their resistance to certain oppressive texts and their affinity for others as manifested in their continual retelling of other biblical texts.[62]

In her 1992 essay "The Hebrew Women Are Not Like the Egyptian Women: The Ideology of Race, Gender and Sexual Reproduction in Exodus 1," Weems does an intersectional reading of Exodus 1, arguing that the story of the Hebrew midwives' encounter with Pharaoh "recasts" an ideology of difference. She states that conflicts around ideologies of difference in the context out of which the text was produced are embedded in the text: difference between Egyptians and Hebrews, women and men, masters and slaves, male and female children, and between Egyptian women and Hebrew women.[63] Weems approaches the text using a literary/narrative and rhetorical reading, paying attention to the narrative voice and ideological perspective embedded in the text that work to persuade the audience of the superiority of the Hebrews to the Egyptians. She focuses on the point of view from which the story is told, which is that of the Hebrew midwives. Weems concludes that the fact that the assumptions or ideologies of difference are not challenged in the text, but exploited to show superiority of Hebrews to Egyptians, would make it difficult to use the text as a liberationist text "without due caution."[64]

The Bible and its stories, viewed as inerrant and infallible texts (usually Eurocentric interpretations of said texts) that re-present nonideological or unbiased truths and narratives, have been presented to Christians, regardless of race, class, gender, or experience, as the *sin qua non* (essential ingredient) for Christian belief and self-understanding. Despite the fact that the Bible's content and interpretations of it have been or remain troubling to many African American women, they have been counseled to cast their cares upon the white Eurocentric Jesus and successive Eurocentric mainstream interpreters/interpretations. African Americans and other peoples of color are admonished and expected to leave the biblical waters untroubled, allowing the

62. Renita J. Weems, "Reading *Her Way* through the Struggle: African American Women and the Bible," in Felder, ed., *Stony the Road We Trod*, 57–79, at 61.
63. Renita Weems, "The Hebrew Women Are Not Like the Egyptian Women: The Ideology of Race, Gender and Sexual Reproduction in Exodus 1," *Semeia* 59 (1992): 25–34.
64. Ibid., 33.

rough, surging waves of oppressive, androcentric interpretations to batter their bodies and souls. Yet, in her SRT essay, "Reading *Her Way* through the Struggle," Weems notes how African American women like Howard Thurman's grandmother evaluated the biblical text based on their normative experience of reality.[65] The pre-experiences or pre-texts of African American women had an impact on how they read. Their pretext for understanding or interacting with the Bible had been a consistent tool in the hands of their oppressors to "restrict and censure" their behavior,[66] as well as their spirit and intellect. African Americans and/or Christians are generally encouraged to read in particular ways, literally or figuratively in ways that conform to church doctrine without regard for the differing historical and cultural contexts between ancient and modern readers.[67] Weems asserts that "Women are taught to think as men, to identify with a male point of view, and to accept as normal and legitimate a male system of values, one of whose principles is misogyny."[68] Black people are expected to read like oppressive white men, and black women to read like oppressed men. But African American women, like Thurman's grandmother, Nancy Ambrose, have "refused to read . . . like a certain kind of man."[69] Unfortunately, however, too many contemporary African American women have and continue to "read the Bible by and large with the eyes of an *oppressed* man!"[70]

All too often, black women have been asked and expected to allow issues of race to trump gender oppression, despite that fact that they experience the world and church as black women and not just as women and not simply as black people. In her SRT essay "The *Haustafeln* (Household Codes) in African American Biblical Interpretation," Clarice Martin calls to task the black church and scholars for focusing on race or slavery in their critical readings of the household codes while ignoring gender subordination. Martin discusses the interpretive history of the household codes among pro-slavery advocates and abolitionists as well as African American approaches to the slave codes within those interpretive contexts.[71] She notes how approaches to the codes calling for wives to submit to husbands differ from those

65. Weems, "Reading *Her Way* through the Struggle," 62.
66. Ibid., 62–63.
67. Ibid., 65.
68. Ibid., 66.
69. Ibid., 67.
70. Ibid., 71.
71. Clarice J. Martin, "The *Haustafeln* (Household Codes) in African American Biblical Interpretation: 'Free Slaves' and 'Subordinate Women,'" in Felder, ed., *Stony the Road We Trod*, 206–31.

to the slave codes. Martin's rationale for writing is based on the significant and extensive negative impact the codes have on African American lives. Offering an internal critique of African American biblical interpreters, Martin argues that they "develop and adopt a liberationist biblical hermeneutic instead of a hierarchalist hermeneutic" concerning interpretation of biblical texts about women and women's positions in public and private spaces.[72] Both black males and females, Martin asserts, should be encouraged to "assume an advocacy stance in identifying liberatory biblical traditions that promote ideological and existential empowerment for black women at every level of ecclesiastical governance."[73] Finally, black women should be encouraged and prepared to enter graduate theological education to take on careers in ordained ministry and to become scholars in religion.[74]

Race matters; gender and class matter. Black women overwhelmingly feel the impact of all three simultaneously as interconnected forms of oppression. African American and womanist biblical interpretation also attempts "to recover the voice of the oppressed within biblical texts," as Renita Weems asserts.[75] Womanist and African American biblical interpretation have argued that the oppressed include those who experience the impact of race, gender, class, and other -isms, and the intersection of these oppressions should be attended to in biblical texts and contexts as well as in the context of African American life.

Not only at the level of narrative and character construction do we uncover the voice of the oppressed but also in the rhetoric and/or language of the text. Martin has argued that language matters, too. In her essay "Womanist Interpretation of the New Testament: The Quest for Holistic and Inclusive Translation and Interpretation," she asserts that it matters, for example, whether we translate the Greek noun *doulos* as "servant" or "slave."[76] The choice to translate *doulos* euphemistically as "servant" masks the socioeconomic and political realities associated with the historical meaning of *doulos* and the function of *doulos* texts in the history of biblical interpretation. Oppressive ideologies rely on language and/or rhetoric to undergird and maintain oppressive systems and institutions, such as patriarchalism, racism, classism, and sexism.

---

72. Ibid., 228.
73. Ibid., 230.
74. Ibid.
75. Weems, "Reading *Her Way* through the Struggle," 73.
76. Clarice J. Martin, "Womanist Interpretations of the New Testament: The Quest for Holistic and Inclusive Translation and Interpretation," *Journal of Feminist Studies in Religion* 6, no. 2 (1990): 41–61.

Critical Self-Reflection

As noted above, African American biblical interpretation was not void of self-reflective critique in the twentieth century. Abraham Smith offered internal critique of African American interpretation as a discipline. Seven years after the publication of STR, he argued for an expansion of its critical dialogue partners, asserting that African American biblical scholars can learn some things from cultural studies as a postmodern critical approach. Similar to Weems and Martin, Smith stated the need to resist an essentialist approach that focuses on race and/or slavery to the exclusion of other critical categories.[77] Other critical categories were not totally absent from the discipline, but Smith's call for an increase in dialogue partners was appropriate.

Similar to Reid and womanist scholars, Smith argued that liberative texts may be both helpful and hurtful; the hurtful elements in biblical texts inscribe patriarchal hegemony. African American biblical hermeneutics should consider an examination of ideals and realities that support hegemony and hegemonic structures, a consideration not lost in Reid's or in a womanist approach. Smith further addresses the need to adopt liberative pedagogy that encourages and engages different voices in dialogue where the teacher learns along with and from their students and vice versa. "To what extent are injustices and exclusions supported or exposed through the various pre-reading, reading, and post-reading practices of biblical interpretation?"[78] Smith, similar to Weems, asserts that "few African American scholars know how to read as 'resisting readers' or how to discern 'textual harassment' because few have had that kind of training."[79] Smith also argues that the adoption of a broad array of reading strategies would assist in avoiding "a rigid perspectivism," allowing them to tread "on ground where the dominant biblical professionals would not expect them to travel in order to avoid the binarism traps of hegemony."[80] For example, when we focus on the racial binary of black and white, we ignore other peoples of color who identify as neither black nor white, reinscribing a socially constructed rigid, simplistic binary. Or when readers limit themselves to the gender binary of heterosexual and homosexual, we silence those who identify as bisexual and transsexual.

77. Abraham Smith, "'I Saw the Book Talk': A Cultural Studies Approach to the Ethics of an African American Biblical Hermeneutics," *Semeia* 77 (1997): 115–38.
78. Ibid., 115.
79. Ibid., 125.
80. Ibid., 126.

African American biblical interpreters must avoid the essentialized black self so as not to perpetuate nonsubversive readings. Smith asserts that "reading with an essentialist notion of self, these early biblical interpreters . . . identified only with the character or values in a text which highlighted one essentialist aspect of their identity."[81] This is the issue that Martin raises when she discusses how scholars have problematized slave regulations in household codes but failed to do the same with the submission of wives to husbands in the same codes. Smith is calling attention to the multiple and complex identities within black communities and that African Americans individually represent or experience. A "reconstructed self" that reads from several perspectives would guard against essentialist readings and myopic perspectivism.

Smith further argues for the need to attend to the "residual voices" and/or views supporting hegemony.[82] It is necessary to maintain a relationship between the most oppressed communities and grassroots, boots-on-the-ground organizations, and to broaden our inner circle of interlocutors. African American biblical interpreters can thereby "gain nourishment from and provide nourishment for subaltern [subordinated] communities . . . so that domination is not perpetuated through an arrogant politics of exclusion or more insidious apologies that justify exclusions" without obtaining spaces that are inclusive.[83] Smith asserts that damaging liberationist biblical texts can be exposed without discarding the texts.[84] African American biblical hermeneutics needs "a comprehensive challenge to hegemony."[85]

Summary

In the twentieth century, African American biblical scholars engaged in black biblical interpretation as a political, subversive act that counteracted and counterperformed, with words and visual art, oppressive Eurocentric readings and images. Biblical interpretation affects and is affected by how we see the world, ourselves, and others in the world. It has an impact on how we relate to or interact with one another and with the earth's resources. Historically and traditionally, the majority of biblical interpreters and interpretations have served the political

81. Ibid., 127.
82. Ibid., 129.
83. Ibid., 130, 131.
84. Ibid., 131.
85. Ibid., 132.

interests of the majority, of (neo)colonizers, and of unbridled capitalism to the detriment of enslaved, indigenous, displaced, exiled, subordinated, (neo)colonized, and poor populations.

Peoples, cultures, and ideologies are prioritized, minimized, or obliterated in the process of and as a result of biblical interpretations. It matters who sets the table (determines the agenda) and who sits at the proverbial table (the invitees). It matters what is included or excluded from the menu and guest list; the two are interconnected. It matters who teaches and what texts they select to be taught. It matters what or whose questions, issues, and concerns are raised, avoided, silenced, treated as marginal, or as (ir)relevant. It matters how we approach and understand the biblical texts (its characters and narratives) and the God about which they testify. African American biblical scholars have not understood the biblical text as a flawless and self-interpreting historical artifact, lacking pretext, context, or bias.

In the twentieth century, African American biblical interpreters utilized various interdisciplinary methods for doing interpretation and did so with various objectives, most notably the recovery of the black presence and relevance for black life. In addition to the exploration and recovery of the African presence, black biblical scholars examined the African American interpretive history, the dilemma of the black seminarian or doctoral student faced with the dominance of Eurocentric biblical interpretation, the significance of "imagination," and the multidimensional experience of black women.

To summarize succinctly, in the twentieth century African American biblical scholars have approached the task of interpretation specifically to achieve the following:

- To deconstruct and counteract racialized ideologically driven Eurocentric biblical interpretations constructed to support the enslavement of black peoples, sexism, classism, and racism;

- To recover the black presence and its significance and/or contribution to biblical stories and texts in order to correct the historical record and to make the historical corrective visually accessible to black readers;

- To determine the function of the black presence in biblical narratives;

- To offer more liberating ways to read the biblical texts and contexts that are relevant to the black community;

47

- To address issues of race, gender, and class in the biblical text and connect it with the experiences and challenges of the black community;

- To demonstrate the importance of language and how it can be used to oppress; and

- To unearth, mine, and reconstruct the history of interpretation among black peoples.

3

African American Biblical Interpretation in the Early Twenty-First Century

As more African American scholars have entered the academy, African American biblical interpretation as an interdisciplinary approach to biblical studies is expanding in terms of sheer numbers and of diverse methods and methodologies employed. Nevertheless, what W. E. B. Du Bois declared to be the problem of the twentieth century continues to be an overarching issue in this century: "the problem of the color line."[1] Race/ethnicity and its mutually impacting social divisions continue to be primary categories of analyses for scholars of color. If it were not for African American interpretation, little, if any, sustained critical engagement about race would likely occur in religious studies, or more specifically in biblical studies. Despite the two-term election of the first black president of the United States, Barack Hussein Obama, the greatest systemic issue facing Americans of color continues to be "the color line" and its intersection with poverty and gender lines.[2] If anyone believed that with Obama's election we had blurred or erased the color line, as his presidency progressed many came to realize how

---

1. Cain Hope Felder, "Introduction," in Felder, ed., *Stony the Road We Trod: African American Biblical Interpretation* (Minneapolis: Fortress Press, 1991), 1–14, at 2.
2. W. E. B. Du Bois, *The Souls of Black Folk* (New York: Bantam, 1989 [1903]).

sadly disillusioned and mistaken they had been. Social media, cell-phone cameras, and globalization all have brought into relief the vicious, life-threatening, predatory nature of racism/classism/sexism/heterosexism and other structural oppressions, including a school-to-prison pipeline and an unparalleled massive prison industrial complex that targets the poor and people of color with annihilating laws and state-sanctioned biased policing, which people of color face daily. The matter of race is evidenced in America's inequitable justice and public-school systems, attempts to roll back civil and voting rights of people of color, and by the hyperracial hostilities directed at our forty-fourth President, Barack Obama and his wife Michelle Obama. Most mainstream, Eurocentric biblical scholars (and scholars of color who have assimilated to the dominant culture) explicitly or implicitly exercise the privilege to ignore and/or rationalize racism and its intersecting -isms while doing biblical interpretation and theological reflection. But many African American biblical scholars continue to live as black people in a racialized and racially hostile world, church, and academy *while* reading. Consequently, African American biblical scholars continue to address racism, classism, sexism, heterosexism, and other -isms as intersecting structures of oppression that have an impact both on them individually and their communities.

Some consider the early publications on the black presence in the Bible by the first African American biblical scholars, like Copher and Felder, as apologetic and even as now irrelevant. Yet black churches and communities continue to embrace their works as a source of powerful positive images of people of color who contributed to the biblical narrative and as a source for combatting internalized racism and its drain on black identity and self-esteem.[3] Race/ethnicity still matters and has a negative impact on the lives of African Americans and other people of color, especially the poor. Black biblical scholars insist, along with critical race theorists,[4] based on lived experiences of minoritized peoples, that racism (and its intersecting realities) is complex; its impact on the lives of the poor, especially on women, their children, and non-cisgendered peoples, can be significantly different. Race remains an important and relevant hermeneutical lens for African Americans and other minoritized persons. As noted in chapter 2, the

3. Cain Hope Felder, *Troubling Biblical Waters: Race, Class, Family* (Maryknoll, NY: Orbis, 1989), xi. As of 1999, it was in its fifteenth printing.
4. See for example, Richard Delgado and Jean Stefancic, *Critical Race Theory. An Introduction,* Second Edition (New York and London: New York University Press, 2012).

intersectionality of race, class, gender, and sexuality describes the hermeneutical framework for womanist and black feminist scholars as well as those scholars who propose to use an African American biblical hermeneutic.

African American biblical scholars continue to expand their inter-disciplinary approaches to interpreting texts, contexts, and readers by increasing their engagement with postcolonial criticism/theories, critical race theories, and cultural studies. They also are expanding their use of cultural artifacts like the rich black literary tradition that includes poetry, novels, slave narratives, and/or spiritual autobiogra-phies; slave songs/spirituals; visual art and film; and lyrics from the blues, rap, rhythm-and-blues, and other contemporary musical genres. African American biblical scholars continue to offer alternative read-ings and approaches to mainstream (primarily white heterosexual males) scholarship that, more than not, ignores and marginalizes other perspectives as irrelevant, illegitimate, unnecessary, and unworthy of engagement. Black biblical scholars raise questions of biblical texts, contexts, cultural readers, and traditions that mainstream Eurocentric biblical scholars might not, do not, and will not ask. Thus, African American biblical scholars contribute a diverse cultural and method-ological creativity to the field of biblical studies and to the task of bib-lical interpretation, tapping into a rich tapestry of cultural traditions, artifacts, contemporary aesthetics, and lived experiences.

At the beginning of the century, Vincent Wimbush challenged black religious scholars generally to foreground African American traditions, culture, experience, and readers as primary texts/contexts. African American experience as the primary lens for reading biblical (con)texts provides a "contrapuntal" (counterpoint) interpretive stance that challenges "the still largely unacknowledged interested, invested, racialized, culture- and ethnic-specific practice of biblical interpre-tation," the larger Eurocentric interpretive tradition in the West to which it belongs.[5] Wimbush calls for the centering of African American experience and, consequently, the decentering of prevailing interpre-tive models, and for understanding the study of the Bible as engage-ment in cultural practice. Wimbush argues that, for African Americans, to read Scripture is to read darkness. "Darkness" refers to an engage-ment with the Bible as a text that "both reflects and draws unto itself

---

5. Vincent L. Wimbush, ed., *African Americans and the Bible: Sacred Texts and Social Textures* (New York/ London: Continuum, 2000), 8. For a fuller definition of "contrapuntal," see Edward Said, *Culture and Imperialism* (New York: Vintage, 1994).

and engages and problematizes a certain complex order of existence associated with marginality, liminality, exile, pain, trauma," resisting the typical and anticipated polarities and dualities.[6] Wimbush challenges readers to allow constructed worlds, cultures, and societies to serve as points of departure and the nitty-gritty of interpretation.

Wimbush's reading darkness (or reading darkly) considers how African Americans have read, but it transcends dark interpretive history and includes contemporary nonminority readers who can consciously choose to read darkly, with a sensibility toward and through the lens of individual and collective trauma. According to Wimbush, anyone can read darkly. Readers that are accustomed to reading from the perspective and position of the dominant culture, from a perch, should first listen and engage with those for whom darkness is indigenous. To "read darkness is to scripturalize and to scripturalize is to read darkness."[7]

Some African American biblical scholars accept that nonAfricana and white peoples can do African American biblical interpretation. However, womanist biblical scholars, as sisters or companions of African American biblical interpretation (but neither subsumed by nor subordinate to it), take the opposite position with regard to who can legitimately do womanist theology or hermeneutics. No *Rachel Dolezaling!*To do African American hermeneutics requires that one read from within a particular lived, existential, ontological reality and/or epistemological vantage points, through which, out of which, and to which God/Goddess speaks and intervenes and to which African Americans bear witness. It is to declare that God also speaks to black peoples through the biblical text and apart from it. Womanist theologians and ethicists like Katie Cannon, Delores Williams, and Jacquelyn Grant have long advocated for prioritizing black women's voices and experiences.[8]

Making the Book Speak: Race, Culture, and Relevance

In this twenty-first century, we have witnessed a proliferation of vol-

6. Wimbush, *African Americans and the Bible*, 17.
7. Ibid., 21. Wimbush's approach is transdisciplinary and not confined to biblical studies. For more about scripturalizing or scripturalization, see Vincent L. Wimbush, *Scripturalizing the Human: The Written as Political* (London/New York: Routledge, 2015); and Wimbush, *White Men's Magic: Scripturalization as Slavery* (New York/London: Oxford University Press, 2012).
8. See, for example, Katie Geneva Cannon, *Katie's Canon: Womanism and the Soul of the Black Community* (New York/London: Bloomsbury, 1998); Jacquelyn Grant, *White Woman's Christ and Black Women's Jesus: Feminist Christology and Womanist Response* (Atlanta: Scholars, 1989); Williams, *Sisters in the Wilderness*.

umes dedicated to the critical reading of entire biblical books/letters or passages through an African American lens and often in dialogue with African American culture, traditions, artifacts, and/or lived realities. This increase is, of course, due to both the growing (and still comparatively very small) numbers of African Americans earning doctoral degrees in biblical studies and the solid body of interpretive work produced in the previous century on which they can build. We are also witnessing a greater openness/acceptance by a few institutions both to the physical presence of black biblical scholars and to the intellectual cultural work such scholars produce that is of relevance to African American communities and to the larger academy and world. Most African American biblical scholars continue to contribute to the discipline of biblical studies by publishing monographs that privilege an African American and/or womanist biblical interpretive approach for reading texts, contexts, and readers. For example, in his book *Then the Whisper Put on Flesh*, Brian Blount reads the Synoptic Gospels, John's Gospel, Pauline letters, and Revelation/the Apocalypse through an African American cultural lens in an attempt to demonstrate the ethical demands for liberation that can be explored within the texts.[9] Blount shows how New Testament texts can be read with the circumstances of oppressed others in view. In his monograph *Can I Get a Witness? Reading Revelation through African American Culture*, Blount argues that a cultural-studies approach to the Apocalypse reveals its meaning for readers who "share its contextual dynamics," clarifying what is obscure and making meaningful that which would be incomprehensible.[10] The objective is to demonstrate points of relevance between the material written for a first-century audience and the twenty-first-century African American community reading it now. As an "organic intellectual" Blount attempts to interpret for a popular audience (especially the one to which he is connected) as well as for the scholarly guild; Blount claims to take a nonelitist approach, "from below" (whether or not he can truly read from below, given his socioeconomic position/place within the academy and in society, is another matter).[11] He asserts that as an interpreter using a cultural-studies approach, he participates in the struggle and does not relegate himself to the sidelines of the struggle. The "cultural studies interpreter not only recognizes

9. Brian K. Blount, *Then the Whisper Put on Flesh: New Testament Ethics in an African American Context* (Nashville: Abingdon, 2001).
10. Brian K. Blount, *Can I Get a Witness? Reading Revelation through African American Culture* (Louisville: Westminster John Knox, 2005), 5.
11. Ibid., 10, 14.

that all readings are culturally and therefore politically contrived; she also realizes that all readings are politically situated."[12] As participant in the struggle and as reader, Blount attempts to construct a reading of Revelation that is "intellectually meaningful and politically transformative for African American Christians and all others who are in community with them."[13] Blount's reading summons the black community to engage in active nonviolent resistance as witnesses. He explores, rhetorically and theologically, two metaphorical images: the martyr and the lamb. Just as the ancient author summoned his audience to participate in their own liberation from oppression, Blount, in his reading of Revelation as and in conversation with resistance literature, issues a similar summons to contemporary African American readers.

Other African American biblical scholars have produced monographs that demonstrate distinct ways of interpreting biblical texts that prioritize cultural relevancy, challenge readings that further oppress communities of color, and critique oppressions within or perpetrated by those communities. New Testament scholars Brad Braxton and Demetrius Williams, respectively, published monographs critiquing the liberation agenda of black preaching through a reading of Galatians, and addressing gender oppression in the black church through an analysis of the Acts of the Apostles.[14] In her book *Call and Consequences*, Raquel St. Clair (Lettsome) reads Mark's Gospel, focusing on the texts in which Jesus summons his disciples (and by extension contemporary readers) to take up their crosses and follow him, thereby exploring the pain/agony/suffering of the Markan Jesus and of black peoples.[15] Following her mentor Brian Blount, St. Clair's interdisciplinary approach includes sociolinguistic theory, which analyzes the social construction of language (the impact of culture, norms, expectations, and context on language). Also building upon the work of womanist theologians like Delores Williams and JoAnne Terrell, St. Clair resists the glorification of suffering in the context of oppression and argues for deconstructing interpretations of Jesus's passion that assist in black women's oppression (and that of others).[16] St. Clair asserts that

12. Ibid., 11–12.
13. Ibid., 36.
14. Brad Ronnell Braxton, *No Longer Slaves: Galatians and African American Experience* (Collegeville, MN: Liturgical/Michael Glazier, 2002); Demetrius K. Williams, *An End to This Strife: The Politics of Gender in African American Churches* (Minneapolis: Fortress Press, 2004).
15. Raquel St. Clair, *Call and Consequences: A Womanist Reading of the Gospel of Mark* (Minneapolis: Fortress Press, 2008).
16. See JoAnne Marie Terrell, *Power in the Blood? The Cross in the African American Experience* (Eugene, OR: Wipf and Stock, 2005).

suffering is a consequence of following one's call, just as Jesus suffered as a result of his ministry. God does not call us, particular black women, to enter into his pain but to partner with him in ministry. Pain, she argues, as recognized, named, and transformed agony (pain and suffering) is a consequence of discipleship or ministry, and not a prerequisite. She asserts that the cross and Jesus's pain were an inevitable consequence of his ministry but were not God's predetermined will; our response to Jesus's call to discipleship inevitably results in pain. St. Clair and others continue to challenge and resist Eurocentric interpretations that ignore the experiences of people of color and, more specifically, black women.

Sixteen years after the publication of *Stony the Road We Trod*, Brian Blount, as general editor, together with associate editors Cain Hope Felder, Clarice Martin, and Emerson Powery, produced the first African American Commentary of the New Testament, *True to Our Native Land: An African American Commentary of the New Testament* (hereafter TONL).[17] In the introduction, Blount acknowledges that "race *still* matters" (emphasis Blount's) as Euro-American interpretive perspectives continue to orient Bible commentaries[18] and biblical studies in general. African American scholars continue to push against the grain as the masses of black people still "stand with their backs against the wall."[19] As Blount argues in TONL, "Minority opinions may be entertained but they are seldom included as resources for any kind of programmatic standardization of rules and regulations . . . they lack political legitimation and, therefore, power."[20] African American biblical interpretation continues to assert that the interpretations of dominant Euro-American biblical scholars "are not more accurate interpretations of biblical texts; they are simply more privileged ones."[21]

TONL also fills a void by providing a text featuring the interpretive works of black biblical scholars that can be included as required reading in New Testament introductory courses. TONL contributes to the ever-expanding repertoire of diverse voices that students and/or readers can access. African American biblical interpretation allows communities of color to hear their own voices, out loud in black-and-white

---

17. Brian K. Blount, gen. ed., with Cain Hope Felder, Clarice J. Martin, and Emerson B. Powery, *True to Our Native Land: An African American Commentary of the New Testament* (Minneapolis: Fortress Press, 2007). Hereafter TONL.
18. Ibid., 1–2.
19. Howard Thurman, *Jesus and the Disinherited* (Boston: Beacon, 1976), 11.
20. Brian L. Blount, Cain Hope Felder, Clarice Martin, and Emerson Powery, "Introduction," in TONL, 1–7, at 3.
21. Ibid., 4.

print. It is also a response to those who use the absence of our voices in print as an excuse for not engaging with diverse, non-Eurocentric voices and perspectives. This does not mean that the black community is always welcoming of their own voices, since many are taught and socialized (in churches, seminaries, divinity schools, and books) to believe that their own concerns are marginal, unnecessary, and even racist, especially when race is prioritized as a category of analysis. Some have been convinced that racism only exists in the minds of radical black people and that it is therefore radical to address issues of race in theological education, and particularly when doing biblical studies. Like many of the dominant culture, too many people of color argue that racism will disappear if we simply stop talking about it; and finally, but not conclusively, some African American Christians adopt an otherworldly view, asserting that racism and other oppressions are better left to God or "when we all get to heaven."

African American scholars continue their commitment to explicitly contextual readings, taking for granted the sacredness and legitimacy of dialogically engaging African American history, traditions, artifacts, and experiences. African American biblical scholars have created and demonstrated intertextualities (bringing together texts to form other texts) between the Scriptures and black culture, traditions, lived experiences, and knowledge production. In my commentary in TONL, I read the Deutero-Pauline letter to the Ephesians in dialogue with the African American experience of "two-ness" or double consciousness as described by W. E. B. Du Bois in his *Souls of Black Folk*. Du Bois states that the "Negro" in America negotiates two existences, one when he is among his own community and one when he interacts with the dominant culture. This black experience of double consciousness (also practiced by other communities of color) means that African Americans "cannot escape the 'sense of always looking at one's self through the eyes of others, of measuring one's soul by the tape of a world that looks on in amused contempt and pity,'" always aware of one's double existence, as both American and black.[22] I argue that the rhetorical construction of the Gentiles in relation to the Jews is very similar to the twoness of the African American experience about which Du Bois wrote. The Gentiles are always referred to as Gentiles and never as Jews, even as they are incorporated into the household of God. They remain Gentiles and are expected to view themselves through Jewish

22. Mitzi J. Smith, "Ephesians," in TONL, 348–62, at 349.

eyes. An intertextuality is unapologetically constructed between Ephesians and African American experience.

Several authors in TONL use similar intertextual and/or dialogical methods in reading other texts. Some readings in TONL are complemented, punctuated, disrupted, and/or intertwined with historical and contemporary parallels, traditions, and other witnesses to African American experience and culture. In Allen Dwight Callahan's reading of John's Gospel, his interpretation of the Nicodemus story and John 3:16 is intertwined with Mary MacLeod Bethune's faith response to the "whosoever believeth" promise of John 3:16 when read by her teacher.[23] Callahan also punctuates his reading with the visual art of African American painter Henry Ossawa Tanner (1859–1937), including his 1899 painting *Nicodemus Visiting Christ* and his 1896 *Resurrection of Lazarus*. In her reading of Luke's Gospel in TONL, Stephanie Buckhanon Crowder sees a congruence between Lukan theology and African American "God talk." For example, Crowder compares and interjects a reading of Mary's song of reversal in celebration of Jesus's birth with Sojourner Truth's bold resistance speech, "Ain't I a Woman?"[24]

This dialogical method is also used in the first African American Hebrew Bible commentary, *The Africana Bible,* which is the First Testament companion to TONL.[25] Hugh Page describes *The Africana Bible* as "an interlocutor with scripture" rather than as a commentary on Scripture; it consists of "critical and impressionistic reflections" on texts deemed sacred by Jewish and Christian readers.[26] The critical reflections arise from the diverse Africana (Africa and the African Diaspora) experience. It is "an invitation to critical reflection on Africana life and the role that the First Testament has played in it."[27] Some contributors to the *Africana Bible* begin their commentaries with brief descriptions of their own social locations and the impact those have on how they read. Scholars like Renita Weems admit their ambivalent locatedness as persons who struggle to construct identities while having roots in Africa *and* America. Weems reads 1–2 Chronicles as a text addressed to an exiled people who find themselves trying to strike a similar balance. As an African American woman with her own memories and experiences, including America's invasion of Iraq in 2003, Weems has a real

---

23. Allen Dwight Callahan, "John," in TONL, 186–212, at 190.
24. Stephanie Buckhanon Crowder, "Luke," in TONL, 158–85.
25. Hugh R. Page Jr., gen. ed., *The Africana Bible: Reading Israel's Scriptures from Africa and the African Diaspora* (Minneapolis: Fortress Press, 2010).
26. Hugh R. Page Jr., "The Africana Bible—A Rationale," in ibid., 3–10, at 3.
27. Ibid., 5.

sense of the chaos into which people are thrown when their cultural memories are nearly decimated. The Chronicler, Weems argues, wants to convince the exiles to return to their homeland but also to make necessary sacrifices to create memories and rebuild monuments with renewed hope.[28]

In his reading of Judges in *The Africana Bible*, Randall Bailey exercises interpretive license by tapping famed black jazz singer and composer Nina Simone's song "Four Women," from which he draws four analytical categories.[29] Simone's "Four Women" addresses social class and gender relative to black women's experiences in the United States as both exploited and agentive persons responding to their oppression. Bailey argues that those experiences relate to the experiences of some women featured in Judges. He hopes to help black communities avoid replicating the ways that women in Judges have been sacrificed by "flawed men." Valerie Bridgeman, in her reading of Jonah, draws upon typical African American preaching traditions on Jonah, Bishop Desmond Tutu's memoir relating to South Africa's Truth and Reconciliation Commission, and Zora Neale Hurston's novel *Jonah's Gourd Vine*.[30] Reading the black preaching tradition together with Jonah, Bridgeman concludes that black sermons have leaned toward "personal piety" and failed to take seriously Jonah's predicament, namely, "how can a people be in relationship with another people who want to destroy them? And, what do we do with Jonah's anger and our quest for justice? . . . Anger provides energy so we may engage in analysis, protest, survival, and justice."[31] Contributors to *The Africana Bible* offer alternative, diverse, relevant, provocative, freedom-loving ways to read biblical texts, critiquing culture, traditions, and artifacts, including the biblical text as sacred artifact. They do not propose to offer the last word or the only alternative for reading sacred texts.

Unlike TONL, *The Africana Bible* rejects the nomenclature of a commentary so as to avoid the impression of a definitive word; it does not claim to provide the only key to the meaning of sacred texts.[32] Indeed, Vincent Wimbush refused to participate as a commentator in TONL, but accepted the invitation to write an essay explaining the reason for his rejection of the commentary as a genre with its claim to offer a final authoritative word. While I agree with Wimbush's assess-

28. Renita Weems, "1–2 Chronicles," in *Africana Bible*, 286–90.
29. Randall C. Bailey, "Judges," in *Africana Bible*, 120–22.
30. Bridgeman, "Jonah," in *Africana Bible*, 183–88.
31. Ibid., 187.
32. Page, ed., *Africana Bible*, 4.

ment of the commentary genre, the fact remains that the majority of pastors, ministers, teachers, and laypersons who study the Bible reach for commentaries and study Bibles as their primary source of authoritative readings for sermon preparation and Bible study. Therefore, it becomes necessary to provide alternative readings that do not require that people of color as readers suspend the questions that arise out of their particular locatedness, based on their race/ethnicity, gender, class, sexual orientation, culture, and other experiences contributing to their intersectional identities.

As with TONL, interpreters use an array of African American artifacts, traditions, aesthetics, and/or witnesses to construct hermeneutical lenses with which to read and dialogue with sacred texts, including historical and modern literary criticisms. African American scholars continue to resist oppressive ideologies found in (con)texts, readers, and readings and to demonstrate how minoritized communities have resisted oppression and hopelessness, recovering that which proves to be a source of encouragement and liberation. In his 2013 book, *Israel's Poetry of Resistance,* Hugh Page creates a space for dialogue between Israel's ancient biblical poetic texts (including some from the book of Psalms and historical books like 2 Samuel) and African American Christianity's use of those texts.[33] Page argues that certain Israelite poems were responses to upheaval, displacement, and marginalization; they are collected and preserved as acts of resistance expressing a collective "no" to the power of despair and an affirmative response to the creative spirit power. They crafted and shaped a future hope that has and can offer a repertoire for African Americans and other marginalized peoples. African American traditions are placed in conversation with ancient poetry, demonstrating the resonance and relevance of Israel's poetry to/for the African American community.

What's in a Name? Constructions of Blackness and Identity

Black biblical scholars, recognizing the significance of constructions of blackness and black people in other ancient texts and contexts, began producing works focusing on ancient literary and rhetorical constructions of black peoples and blackness outside of, but not excluding, the two canonical testaments. In *Symbolic Blackness and Ethnic Difference in Early Christian Literature,* Gay Byron examines the discursive use of Egypt/Egyptian, Ethiopia/Ethiopian, and black/blackness through

---

33. Hugh R. Page Jr., *Israel's Poetry of Resistance* (Minneapolis: Fortress Press, 2013).

ethno-political rhetorics, arguing that the images of black/blackness came to represent extremes within early Christianity.[34] In her 2009 essay, "Ancient Ethiopia and the New Testament: Ethnic (Con)texts and Racialized (Sub)texts," Byron argues for the need to identify and analyze "racialized (sub)texts in the ancient texts" as well as race and racism operative in contemporary (sub)texts when interpreting biblical texts and contexts. Such an interpretive departure point can raise questions regarding the ethnic (con)texts from which ancient texts emerged.[35] Byron's work continues to challenge biblical scholars to expand the geographical frame of reference for understanding New Testament texts and contexts. Her current work centers on translating/interpreting New Testament manuscripts written in Ge'ez (an ancient Semitic language that survives today as the liturgical language of the Ethiopian Orthodox Church and is the ancestral language of modern Ethiopian dialects) and articulating their importance for understanding early Christianity and its texts.[36]

Wil Gafney's essay in *The Africana Bible*, entitled "Reading the Hebrew Bible Responsibly," calls attention to the impact of race/ethnicity, gender, and religious identity on language construction within the text and in translations/interpretations of the text's language. Gafney argues that one can find liberation or oppression in a name. "Responsible exegesis of the scriptures of Israel requires respect for and fidelity toward the Semitic languages, peoples, and cultures of the scriptures of Israel," which means that we cease to mediate the Scriptures through "gentilic languages, especially German."[37] This same linguistic laziness that many readers exhibit toward biblical names and language we find practiced in contemporary societies toward unique racial/ethnic names. As Gafney argues, "the multicultural nature of Israel is especially important to read over and against racialized constructions of Israel as ethnically and racially monolithic, and their construction as 'white' in the nineteen and twentieth centuries."[38]

---

34. Gay H. Byron, *Symbolic Blackness and Ethnic Difference in Early Christian Literature: Blackened by the Skins* (New York: Routledge, 2002). See also Rodney Sadler, *Can a Cushite Change His Skin? An Examination of Race, Ethnicity and Othering in the Hebrew Bible* (New York/London: Bloomsbury/T&T Clark, 2009).

35. Gay Byron, "Ancient Ethiopia and the New Testament: Ethnic (Con)texts and Racialized (Sub)texts," *They Were All Together in One Place? Toward Minority Biblical Criticism*, ed. Randall C. Bailey, Tat-Siong Benny Liew, and Fernando F. Segovia, Semeia Studies 57 (Atlanta: SBL Press, 2009), 161–90, at 180.

36. See also Gay L. Byron, "Black Collectors and Keepers of Tradition: Resources for a Womanist Biblical Ethic of (Re)Interpretation," in *Expanding the Discourse of Womanist Hermeneutics*, ed. Gay L. Byron and Vanessa Lovelace, Semeia Studies 85 (Atlanta: SBL Press, 2016), 187–208.

37. Wil Gafney, "Reading the Hebrew Bible Responsibly," in *Africana Bible*, 48.

Intersectionality: Race/Ethnicity, Gender, Class, and Sexuality

In the twenty-first century, African American biblical scholars increasingly address the complexity of social divisions, oppression, and individual lived experience. Womanist and black feminist theologians and ethicists have long insisted upon intersectional analysis, using terms like "interlocking," "multidimensional," and "intersecting" (i.e., the impact of interconnected forms of oppression and/or identities).[39] Intersectionality is understood as a means of analysis that allows one to examine how power relations are interconnected. It includes categories like race/ethnicity, class, gender, sexuality, dis/ability, nation/empire, religion, and age that signify social divisions which "gain meaning from power relations of racism, sexism, heterosexism, and class exploitation."[40] Patricia Hill Collins and Sirma Bilge provide the following general definition of intersectionality:

> A way of understanding and analyzing the complexity in the world, in people, and in human experiences. The events and conditions of social and political life and the self can seldom be understood as shaped by one factor. They are generally shaped by many factors in diverse and mutually influencing ways. When it comes to social inequality, people's lives and the organization of power in a given society are better understood as being shaped not by a single axis of social division, be it race or gender or class, but by many axes that work together and influence each other. Intersectionality as an analytic tool gives people better access to the complexity of the world and of themselves.[41]

While African American male theologians and biblical scholars have always insisted on race as a category of analysis, black feminist and womanist scholars as theologians, ethicists, and biblical scholars have most consistently insisted on a critical analysis that considers race, gender, and class, and, more recently, sexuality. In 2009, Randall Bailey published an essay titled "'That's Why They Didn't Call the Book Hadassah!': The Interse(ct)/(x)ionality of Race/Ethnicity, Gender, and Sexuality in the Book of Esther," using narrative and ideological criticism to examine how the narrator characterizes the Persian king, the king's eunuchs, Haman, the Jewish virgin Esther, and Mordecai (Esther's Jew-

---

38. Ibid., 49.
39. See, for example, Kelly Brown Douglas, *Sexuality and the Black Church: A Womanist Perspective* (Maryknoll, NY: Orbis, 1999).
40. Patricia Hill Collins and Sirma Bilge, *Intersectionality* (Malden, MA/Cambridge, UK: Polity, 2016), 7.
41. Ibid., 7.

ish uncle) in relationship to each other.[42] Modern commentators, unfortunately, have embraced the ideology of the text that privileges one ethnic group above another. Sexuality and sexual practices (intersecting with ethnicity) are employed to negatively signify the "other" (the Persians) in order to legitimize Israelite oppression of the other. But Esther is also sexualized (based on patriarchal ideology transcending ethnicity); she wins the king's favor by "sexing the King better than anyone else [based on the experiential advice she received from the King's eunuch Hegai]"; she is commodified.[43] Although the sexualizing tendencies in the narrative are not concealed by the text, they are basically ignored by interpreters in the secondary literature. Bailey argues that the use of what he calls "cover-up translations" that prefer euphemisms to direct, harsh, offensive, and/or realistic expressions lessen the chance of recognizing seduction motifs in Esther and in other texts like Ruth.[44]

In his essay "'Upon All Flesh': Acts 2, African Americans and Intersectional Realities," Demetrius Williams, like Bailey, uses both ideological and narrative criticism to explore the ideologies that are operating in support of the author's narrative strategy.[45] He attends to the ideologies so as not to replicate the perspective of the text or the author's agenda. Williams's ultimate goal is to place Luke's strategy in conversation with the function and interpretive history of the Acts 2 prophecy among African Americans. Williams argues that "Acts provides a deficient model of inclusivity."[46] Racial-ethnic inclusivity was practiced in accordance with the diverse ethic inclusivity of the Roman Empire, which could be embraced without upsetting the conventional and hierarchical social status quo. Thus, Williams argues that "Luke upholds Roman values of virtus and imperium, which encompasses the

---

42. Randall Bailey, "'That's Why They Didn't Call the Book Hadassah!': The Interse(ct)/(x)ionality of Race/Ethnicity, Gender, and Sexuality in the Book of Esther," in Bailey, Liew, and Segovia, eds., *They Were All Together in One Place?*, 227–50.

43. Ibid., 239.

44. Ibid., 240–41. In his article, "The Cushite in David's Army Meets Ebedmelek: The Impact of Supremacist Ideologies on the Interpretations and Translations of Texts," in *Samuel Read through Different Eyes: The Collected Writings of Randall C. Bailey* (Grand Rapids: Eerdmans, forthcoming), Bailey returns to his earlier Afrocentric biblical interpretation model presented in his 2000 article "Academic Biblical Interpretation among African Americans in the United States" (in Wimbush, ed., *African Americans and the Bible*, 696–711), and contours how the history of white supremacist interpretations of the Cushite in 2 Samuel 18 and the translations of *saris* in Jeremiah 38 have continued to plague Eurocentric biblical interpretation, seeing the Cushite in Samuel as a slave and Ebed-Melek as a castrated individual, and ignoring the clues that these characters are narratively presented as highly valued military strategists.

45. Demetrius K. Williams, "'Upon All Flesh': Acts 2, African Americans and Intersectional Realities," in Bailey, Liew, and Segovia, eds., *They Were All Together in One Place?*, 289–310.

46. Ibid., 302.

virtues of social order and masculinity. Therefore, Luke does not depict women and slaves engaging in powerful speech and behavior contrary to Roman social values, showing just how closely he comports to elite male values."[47] Black males in early twentieth-century African American religious history, particularly those in the early Pentecostal movement, limited their interpretation of the Joel prophecy in Acts to racial, ethnic barriers. However, nineteenth-century black women like Zilpha Elaw, Julia Foote, and Rosa Horn (in the early twentieth century) saw such interpretation as removing barriers to both race and gender. The text was used to argue for inclusive and just acts in society and church. Williams notes that "African American women's historical experience has compelled them to consider the intersectional realities of race, ethnicity, class/status, and sex/gender."[48] As traditionally expected, Williams explicates the text first, addresses the African American tradition second, and, finally, applies his textual analysis to the contemporary African American context.

Some of the most significant contributions to biblical studies and to African American biblical interpretation have come from African American biblical scholars doing womanist biblical interpretation. This century has witnessed an unprecedented number of publication of monographs and essays authored by black female biblical scholars. As mentioned above, Raquel St. Clair (Lettsome) published her monograph entitled *Call and Consequences* in 2009. Since then, womanist biblical scholars have increasingly addressed issues of intersectionality, taking into consideration the complexity of their own social location as black women religious scholars. New Testament scholars Shanell Teresa Smith and Lynne St. Clair Darden have published seminal book-length womanist readings of Revelation.[49] Smith and Darden read Revelation through womanist interpretive interdisciplinary lenses that engage both cultural studies and postcolonial theories (e.g., Homi Bhabha's theory of hybridity and ambivalence). Smith brings together Bhabha's *ambivalence* with Du Bois's *veil* and coins the term "ambiveilence" as a lens for reading the woman Babylon, who is

---

47. Ibid.
48. Ibid., 307.
49. Shanell T. Smith, *The Woman Babylon and the Marks of Empire: Reading Revelation with a Postcolonial Womanist Hermeneutics of Ambiveilence*, Emerging Scholars (Minneapolis: Fortress Press, 2015); Lynne St. Clair Darden, *Scripturalizing Revelation: An African American Postcolonial Reading of Empire* (Atlanta: SBL Press, 2015). For a womanist essay on Revelation, see Clarice Martin, "Polishing the Unclouded Mirror: A Womanist Reading of Revelation 18:13," in *From Every People and Nation: The Book of Revelation in Intercultural Perspective*, ed. David Rhoads (Minneapolis: Fortress Press, 2005): 82–109.

described as both slave woman and queen. The complexity of our social locations and experiences allows Smith to identity with both descriptions of the woman Babylon. Smith and Darden produce readings of Revelation that take into account the complexity and diversity of black women's lives and black people's experiences. They consider issues of class, gender, race, and empire. Like Blount's reading of Revelation, Smith and Darden spend considerable space laying out and explaining the theoretical frameworks and methods while their final chapters are dedicated to applying those theories.[50]

Margaret Aymer's essay "Outrageous, Audacious, Courageous, Willful: Reading the Enslaved Girl of Acts 12" reads Rhoda's story intersectionally, darkly, and ambiv*eil*ently (Shanell Smith's term). Aymer reads through her own particularity and privilege, recognizing that both complicity and resistance co-exist in her body, as reader. By allowing the silenced Rhoda to speak, Aymer addresses Rhoda's trauma caused by the darkness of intersectional oppressions of racism/ethnocentrism, sexism, classism, and ageism (youth).[51] Aymer further challenges Luke's romanticized view of women and disrupts the narrative with Rhoda's presence. In my forthcoming book, titled *Womanist Sass and Back Talk: Social (In)Justice, Intersectionality, and Biblical Interpretation* (Cascade, 2017), I interpret biblical (con)texts through a womanist lens that foregrounds contemporary social justice issues and the interconnectedness of race/ethnicity, gender, class, and (neo)colonialism. The womanist social justice framework addresses issues related to my immediate lived-teaching context in the Detroit metro area and in the world. For example, I read the story of Jesus's encounter with the Samaritan woman at the well in John's Gospel through and in conversation with the water shut-offs in Detroit, Michigan. My hermeneutical lens engages postcolonial and political science theories (e.g., ambivalence, stereotypes, and a politics of disgust). I focus on the impact of the crisis on poor women of color, their families, and their communities. Other essays in the volume prioritize social justice issues such as police brutality and violence against poor black women. African Ameri-

50. I agree with Michael Joseph Brown's criticism of Blount's cultural reading of Revelation (Can I Get a Witness?: Reading Revelation through African American Culture, *The Journal of Religion* 86 no. 2 [2006]: 306–8) wherein he states that Blount should spend more time applying the methodology rather than discussing it.

51. Margaret Aymer, "Outrageous, Audacious, Courageous, Willful: Reading the Enslaved Girl of Acts 12," in Byron and Lovelace, eds., *Expanding the Discourse of Womanist Hermeneutics*, 265–90. See also Bridgett Green, "Nobody's Free until Everybody's Free': Exploring Gender and Class Injustice in a Story about Children (Luke 18:15-17)," in Byron and Lovelace, eds., *Expanding the Discourse of Womanist Hermeneutics*, 291–310.

can and womanist biblical interpretation continue to challenge biblical studies to produce interpretations that are culturally and theologically relevant, reflecting the concerns of and accessible to the most marginalized among us. In my essay titled "Race, Gender, and the Politics of 'Sass': Reading Mark 7:24-30 through a Womanist Lens of Intersectionality and Inter(con)textuality," I read the story of Jesus's encounter with the Syrophoenician woman through the womanist lens of black women's "sass/talk back" as resistance language, a mother tongue, and *heteroglossia* (Mikhail Bakhtin's term), as demonstrated in Sandra Bland's story (the black female motorist whose arrest ended in death in a Texas jail in 2015).[52] African American biblical interpretation, like all biblical interpretation, is political, seeking to expose oppressive ideologies in texts, contexts, and in ancient and contemporary readers and readings. This political agenda includes the debunking of respectability politics, which claims that people of color and poor people will always be treated with dignity, justice, and respect in a racialized, patriarchal, and class-conscious society when they exhibit acceptable behaviors. Unacceptable behaviors, according to a politics of respectability, like responding to injustice or resisting and protesting systemic racism, sexism, and violence from authority figures, should result in negative, harmful outcomes, particularly when the actors are persons of color.

Stephanie Crowder's book *When Momma Speaks* explores race, gender, and motherhood from a womanist perspective. Crowder explores historical ideas about motherhood within the African American community and their impact on contemporary black culture. With African American culture in view, Crowder interprets biblical stories about mothers like Bathsheba, Hagar, and the Canaanite woman, demonstrating how they are significant sources for empowerment, critical reflection, and identification.[53]

There's a Problem with the Text

As demonstrated above, African American biblical scholars increasingly acknowledge and address the "elephant in the room" or in the (con)text, affirming what many of our African ancestors previously contended: sometimes there's a problem with the biblical (con)text

52. Mitzi J. Smith, "Race, Gender, and the Politics of 'Sass': Reading Mark 7:24-20 through a Womanist Lens of Intersectionality and Inter(con)textuality," in Byron and Lovelace, eds., *Expanding the Discourse of Womanist Hermeneutics*, 95–112.
53. Stephanie Buckhanon Crowder, *When Momma Speaks: The Bible and Motherhood from a Womanist Perspective* (Louisville: Westminster John Knox, 2016).

itself. The biblical text is not synonymous with God. This hermeneutical intuition and revelation was not a theological stumbling block nor did it threaten our African Ancestors' faith in God, Jesus Christ, or the Holy Spirit. Critical engagement with the Scriptures could involve a resistance to and/or a rejection of some biblical texts and yet leave "my Jesus" intact. Despite biblical texts that plainly decree, for example, that slaves ought to obey their masters, Jesus was a liberator God. Following the tradition of their African ancestors, African American biblical scholars continue to confront and challenge oppressive ideologies and theologies inscribed in the biblical (con)/(sub)texts themselves. For example, in his 2005 essay titled "Canaanites, Cowboys, and Indians," Bailey, embracing the role of an ideological critic, admits that the problem just might be with the text itself.[54] Rather than reading the Joshua 1–12 conquest narratives using Pentateuchal source criticism, Randall reads the narratives in their final form, as the ordinary reader receives it. He argues that "we must engage the text in order to be clear on why we are resisting it."[55] The story of the natives is told by their conquerors, resulting in disturbing ideological constructions of the "indigenes for the aggrandizement of the conqueror."[56] The stories of Rahab, the Gibeonites, and the kings of the South admonish native peoples to become traitors to their own people and to position themselves on the side of their conquerors, those who confiscate their lands. They do so by negotiating with their conquerors, adhering to their religion, serving their god, and assisting them. The ideological strategy revealed in the text is trifold: sexualize the indigenes; dismantle their religion and religious shrines; destroy their intellectual property. Ideological problems exist in the biblical text itself, including the construction of God as dispossessor, desecrator, and dehumanizer of other peoples.[57]

African American biblical scholars have demonstrated the importance of questioning the normative, taken-for-granted reading of a text that requires readers to side with elite male perspectives, with the Israelites over against those considered foreigners, with those least like us, as opposed to those who are othered in the text. Thus, African

---

54. Randall C. Bailey, "He Didn't Even Tell Us the Worst of It!" *Union Seminary Quarterly Review* 59, no. 1 (2005): 15–27. See Robert Warrior, "Canaanites, Cowboys, and Indians: Canaanites, Cowboys and Indians," in *Voices from the Margins: Interpreting the Bible in the Third World*, ed. R. S. Sugirtharajah (London: SPCK, 1991), 287–95.
55. Bailey, "He Didn't Even Tell Us the Worst of It!," 16.
56. Ibid., 17.
57. Ibid., 20–24.

American biblical scholars have analyzed the connection between nation building, gender/sexuality, class, and the racialized other in ancient and contemporary contexts.[58] Cheryl Anderson's essay "Reflections in an Interethnic/Racial Era on Interethnic/Racial Marriage in Ezra" compares the exclusionary policies in the book of Ezra with those that banned interracial marriage in America's segregationist era and that continue to affect us today.[59] Reading Ezra as a "cautionary tale," Anderson argues that Ezra's intermarriage ban constructs both group religious identity and differences based on ethnicity/race (which she argues are not inherently different concepts), class, and gender; such distinctions later function as sacred precedents employed against African Americans with disastrous consequences. Such distinctions are similar to those employed during America's segregationist era and beyond. Anderson states that "accepting the apparent rationale [for excluding foreigners] means that excluding those who are different can be warranted, and critical questions about the group identity to be preserved and the impact on those excluded, as experienced in our own past, are obscured."[60] That prohibition constructs both a group religious identity and differences based on ethnicity/race, class, and gender in the biblical text. Modern readers are urged to take seriously the social and historical contexts of both the contemporary reading community and of the biblical text. Anderson argues that interracial bans in the Persian Yehud (Jerusalem) and in America's segregationist period served the interests of the privileged; the history of African Americans is one largely of being disadvantaged by the privileged.[61] African Americans cannot afford to ignore and fail to critically engage exclusionary tendencies and constructions of difference in the biblical text that benefit a privileged segment of society. Anderson states that we cannot afford to ignore our past or our present when we open the biblical text.

---

58. In terms of the New Testament, scholars like Monya Stubbs (*Indebted Love: Paul's Subjection Language in Romans* [Eugene, OR: Wipf and Stock, 2013]) has addressed economic and political dominance in ancient Rome and contemporary society in thinking about obligations and mutuality of love. Comparing African American perspectives and the apostle Paul in Romans, Stubbs argues that human beings will inherently exist in a condition of submission but the goal is to submit to God's power and seek freedom from evil powers.

59. Cheryl B. Anderson, "Reflections in an Interethnic/Racial Era on Interethnic/Racial Marriage in Ezra," in Bailey, Liew, and Segovia, eds., *They Were All Together in One Place?*, 47–64, at 61. See also Madeline McClenney-Sadler, "Cry Witch: The Embers Still Burn," in *Pregnant Passion, Gender, Sex and Violence in the Bible*, ed. Cheryl A. Kirk-Duggan, Semeia Studies 44 (Atlanta: SBL Press, 2003), 116–41.

60. Anderson, "Reflections on an Interethnic-Racial Era," 47.

61. Ibid., 47–53.

Yolanda Norton would agree with Anderson that people of color, and particularly black women, cannot ignore how biblical texts can encourage readers to ignore their own histories and present circumstances. In her essay titled "Silenced Struggles for Survival: Finding Life in Death in the Book of Ruth," Norton reads the book of Ruth through the womanist lens of the trope of the "strong black woman."[62] She argues that Ruth functions to affirm normative power structures that negatively impact black women and other women of color; it promotes the superiority of Israel over non-Israelites. Ruth forsakes her own culture, country, and biological family; she assimilates, takes risks, and makes sacrifices so that Naomi might survive and have an heir. In the book's reception history, white male norms have been overtly and covertly prescribed to the disadvantage of black women. Norton argues that the story of Ruth has served as a mimetic paradigm of the woman who risks her own health to serve as the care-taker and surrogate for others.

An inherent part of Bible translations that scholars seldom address is the impact of subtitles that carry significant hermeneutical weight and influence how readers read or fail to read biblical passages. The subtitles that are inscribed in Bibles often persuade and/or guide readers to understand pericopae in one particular way, making it difficult for them to read the text differently from the way the dominant culture and/or mainstream Eurocentric interpreters read and in ways that reinscribe irrelevant and/or oppressive theologies and ideologies. In *Teaching All Nations: A Womanist Interrogation of the Matthew Great Commission,* which I co-edited with Lalitha Jayachitra, we bring together three female biblical scholars (two African American and one Asian South Indian) to provide critical readings of Matthew 28:16–20, putatively and iconically recognized as the "Great Commission."[63] In my essay titled "'Knowing More than Is Good for One': Interrogating the Matthean Great Commission," I read Matthew 28:16–20 using a womanist interpretive lens to address the hermeneutical problem caused by the iconic labeling and the oppressive impact of the "Great Commission" that encouraged and continues to promote the subordination of social justice to teaching.

62. Yolanda Norton, "Silenced Struggles for Survival: Finding Life in Death in the Book of Ruth," in *I Found God in Me*, 265–79.
63. Mitzi J. Smith and Lalitha Jayachitra, eds., *Teaching All Nations: Interrogating the Matthew Great Commission* (Minneapolis: Fortress Press, 2014).

Corrective Reconstruction and Reimagining for Freedom

African American and womanist biblical scholars have sometimes had to reconstruct or reimagine a concept or text in order to produce a relevant, legitimizing, and liberating reading of a biblical text. In doing so, they often hope to construct the intellectual and spiritual space for seeing and reading biblical texts and characters in ways that expose and critique patriarchy, misogyny, and elitism inscribed in them. For example, Hebrew Bible scholar Kimberly Russaw, in her essay titled "Wisdom in the Garden," notes that women are not called wise in the Hebrew Bible.[64] Therefore, she reconstructs the markers of a wise person from the biblical text and other ancient texts that encourage or allow readers to imagine Eve as a wise woman. The wise, crafty serpent finds Eve to be a worthy dialogue partner who eats the fruit of the tree of good and evil only after considering her options. Eve pursues wisdom, as wise people are apt to do. Russaw writes that "the story of this woman can be read in such a way that those heretofore relegated to the margins of wisdom and wisdom literature because of their gender (and perhaps their race, class, or sexual orientation) might find themselves closer to the center of the text."[65] Russaw finally compares Eve's wisdom with the wisdom demonstrated by the womanist character Sophia Butler in Alice Walker's novel *The Color Purple*. Her "reading challenges the affinity of many in and outside the academy to relegate wisdom, its literature, and its characters to prescribed portions of the biblical canon and in so doing expand our critical inquiry beyond the bounds of what may be considered safe, or even good for us."[66]

In her womanist midrash on Zipporah, Wil Gafney attempts to maintain the characters' names in their ethnic form as a sign of respect. She interprets biblical and rabbinic literature about the story of Moshe (Moses) and Tzipporah (Zipporah), prioritizing the experience of black women. Gafney recovers Zipporah as an African woman whose character functions in a multiplicity of roles, including as a motherless daughter, clergy spouse, divorcee, shepherd, survivor, and matriarch. Zipporah, Gafney argues, "transcends and transforms stereotypes" that

64. Kimberly Russaw, "Wisdom in the Garden. The Woman of Genesis 3 and Alice Walker's *Sophia*," in *I Found God in Me: A Womanist Biblical Hermeneutics Reader*, ed. Mitzi J. Smith (Eugene, OR: Cascade, 2015), 222–34. See also Febbie Dickerson, "Acts 9:36–43: The Many Faces of Tabitha, A Womanist Reading," in *I Found God in Me: A Womanist Biblical Hermeneutics Reader*, ed. Mitzi J. Smith (Eugene, OR: Cascade, 2015), 297–312, where she rescues Tabitha/Dorcas from conventional stereotypical readings of her as the helpful powerless widow whose presence elevates Peter.
65. Ibid., 231.
66. Ibid., 234.

are often applied to black women.[67] Because naming is meaningful and some significant biblical women's identities are suppressed in the text, Gafney imaginatively constructs a name for Zipporah's six sisters (Liya, Aminah, Minnah, Taima, Yarah, and Zizah) and their mother (Poriyah).

Expanding the Protestant Canon

Seventeenth- to early-nineteenth-century King James Version Bibles contained Christian apocryphal texts. Enslaved Africans, like the early-nineteenth-century slave, Nat Turner, who led a slave revolt in 1831, may have accessed the content of apocryphal texts like Tobit or Enoch.[68] Many African American Christians reject apocryphal texts as sacred while some of their African ancestors may have found them inspirational. *The Africana Bible* demonstrates that deuterocanonical and/or pseudepigraphical texts can also be read using an African American hermeneutic. In his reading of 1 Enoch, Hugh Page cites an affinity between Africana religious experience and the book of 1 Enoch; they both demonstrate the significance of oral and written visionary experiences and traditions, including special revelations and dreams, which are considered normative and emerging from the "sanctified imagination" or divine inspiration.[69] Adam Stokes notes the parallels between the black American folkloric "trickster" characters that use wisdom to conquer a powerful enemy and the Bel and the Dragon narrative (a Greek addition to Daniel).[70] In her reading of Susanna (also a Greek addition to Daniel), Stacy Davis sees the character of Susanna as "a model for oppressed Africana women, who are often forced to be silent but who know when a timely word can lead to their redemption."[71] Further, Davis argues that had Africana women constructed the narrative, a woman, and not Daniel, "would have been another woman's savior."[72]

67. Wil Gafney, "A Womanist Midrash of Zipporah," in Smith, ed., *I Found God in Me*, 131–57, at 131. See also Gafney, *Womanist Midrash: A Reintroduction to the Women of the Torah and Throne* (Louisville: Westminster John Knox, 2017).
68. Allen Callahan, *The Talking Book: African Americans and the Bible* (New Haven: Yale University Press, 2006).
69. Page, "1 Enoch," in *Africana Bible*, 328–30.
70. Adam Oliver Stokes, "Bel and the Dragon," in *Africana Bible*, 314–15.
71. Stacy Davis, "Susanna," in *Africana Bible*, 312.
72. Ibid., 313.

History of Interpretation and Decentering the Biblical Text

African American biblical scholars have broadened their cultural exploration of the interpretive history of texts and biblical events by black peoples from the antebellum period through the civil rights movement era and beyond. Doing biblical studies unapologetically includes engaging cultural studies and a decentering of the biblical text while privileging African Americans as interpreters or producers of sacred epistemologies. They analyze how black people have interpreted biblical texts, events, and images and how they functioned in their contexts and lives to legitimize, encourage hope, and liberate them and their communities. In his 2006 monograph *The Talking Book*, Allen Callahan analyzes the various functions of the Bible among enslaved and free black peoples in America, arguing that it functioned simultaneously as a talking book, a poison book, and a good book.[73] Callahan also examines the significance of the biblical interpretive motifs of exile, exodus, Ethiopia, and Emmanuel among African Americans.

Margaret Aymer's book *First Pure, then Peaceable: Frederick Douglass Reads James* examines how nineteenth-century abolitionist and former slave Frederick Douglass read the epistle of James, particularly verse 3:17.[74] Following Wimbush, she calls it a darkness reading, reading through the darkness of his circumstances. Aymer decenters the biblical text, placing Douglass as reader at the center of her analysis.

Some African American biblical scholars continue to decenter the Bible as the primary text for doing biblical studies and/or interpretation. In my 2011 interdisciplinary essay "'Unbossed and Unbought': Zilpha Elaw and Old Elizabeth and Political Discourse of Origins," I examine black women's spiritual autobiographies to show how nineteenth-century black preaching women interpreted Pauline biblical texts in light of their own contexts of divine revelation and gender oppression in order to construct a discourse of political origins legitimizing their calls to public preaching ministry.[75] Rather than reject the Pauline Scriptures, as Nancy Ambrose (Howard Thurman's grandmother) had, they borrowed images and language from the Pauline call and Damascus Road narratives for their own purposes. In another essay

---

73. Callahan, *The Talking Book.*
74. Margaret Aymer, *First Pure, then Peaceable: Frederick Douglass Reads James* (New York: T&T Clark, 2008).
75. Mitzi J. Smith, "'Unbossed and Unbought': Zilpha Elaw and Old Elizabeth and Political Discourse of Origins," *Black Theology* 9, no. 3 (2011): 287–311.

titled "Give Me Jesus: Salvation History in the Spirituals," I analyze the African American cultural tradition of the slave songs/spirituals (complemented with slave narratives) to demonstrate how the enslaved hermeneutically articulated a salvation history, which I place in dialogue with Hans Conzelmann's conceptualization of *Heilsgeschichte* (salvation history).[76] New Testament scholar Stephanie Buckhanon Crowder explores the use of New Testament themes, images, and language in popular music by African American artists, particularly the music of Prince, Lauryn Hill, and Kanye West. Crowder argues that within African and African American culture we find a long and rich history demonstrating and celebrating a fluidity between a later infused dichotomy between the sacred and the profane. But what we find in popular music is dismissal of or crossing of that boundary, a blending of the sacred and secular. For example, in his song "Jesus Walks," Kanye West's hermeneutical license renders Jesus as a Jesus of the people, a Savior available to all, including "hustlers, killers, murderers, drug dealers, strippers, and victims of welfare."[77] Reading the work of mystical cultural icon and theologian Howard Thurman, New Testament scholar Thomas Slater argues that Thurman was the forerunner of the Third Quest for the historical Jesus, as articulated in Thurman's book *Jesus and the Disinherited*. Thurman develops the argument that we cannot understand Jesus apart from his Jewishness and his sociohistorical context as one living under the Roman Empire; that Jesus was a poor, oppressed, Jewish peasant who identified with other marginalized persons.[78] In fact, Thurman aptly asserts that if the apostle Paul and Jesus fell into a ditch, Jesus would just be a "Jew" in a ditch, but Paul would be a Roman citizen in a ditch. Yet Thurman's contribution was ignored by the academy for several reasons: he was African American; he did not earn an academic doctoral degree in New Testament studies; he did not adhere to the myth of objectivity; he did not teach at an Ivy League school; and he wrote to "inspire the uninspired."[79]

Two recent books continue the project of cultural studies focusing on how enslaved and free African Americans interpreted Scripture and its function in their lives and contexts, and in the oral and written

---

76. Mitzi J. Smith, "Give Me Jesus: Salvation History in the Spirituals," in *Afrocentric Interpretations of Jesus and the Gospel Tradition: Things Black Scholars See That White Scholars Overlook*, ed. Thomas Bowie Slater (Lewiston, NY: Edwin Mellen, 2015), 57–88.
77. Stephanie Buckhanon Crowder, "The New Testament of R&B," in *Afrocentric Interpretations of Jesus*, 19–36, at 33.
78. Thomas B. Slater, "Howard Thurman: His Influence and His Relationship to the Third Quest," in *Afrocentric Interpretations of Jesus*, 37–55.
79. Ibid., 55.

works they constructed. Hebrew Bible scholar Herbert Marbury argues in his 2015 book *Pillars of Cloud and Fire* that the phrases "pillars of cloud" and "pillars of fire" function as metaphors for the diverse and double interpretive typologies describing African Americans' articulations of the exodus event for engendering social transformation.[80] Marbury argues that "pillar of cloud performances" are characterized by a doubling that both conceals like a mask "the existential alienation that African Americans experience as a part of everyday life" and also advertises or feigns contentment with the oppressive social context. The wearing of the mask or the hiding is accomplished through the mastery of socially and politically acceptable conduct (e.g., virtues of manhood, womanhood, and morality, exemplary citizenship, intellectual prowess), giving the impression of congruity with the social world. Thus, they avert attention away from what lies behind the mask. Those black interpreters who represent pillars of fire reject the mask so as to advertise their displeasure and incongruence with an unjust social order; their political capital is based on their refusal to fit in.[81] New Testament scholar Emerson Powery and Hebrew Bible scholar Rodney Sadler's 2015 book titled *The Genesis of Liberation* explores how the Bible functioned among the enslaved, as articulated in slave narratives of, for example, Frederick Douglass, William J. Anderson, and Linda Brent.[82] The use of the Bible as both a tool of oppression and suppression as well as inspiration further ignited in the enslaved Africans a strong desire to learn to read in order to read the Bible and to read the Bible in order to learn to read. Hearing, memorizing, and reading certain Scriptures for themselves encouraged slave resistance (physical and intellectual) and other forms of agency. Powery and Sadler focus on the reception and use of Scripture among the antebellum enslaved.

Moving Forward

While African American biblical interpretation has always been an interdisciplinary endeavor, I believe it will continue on the path of seeking new dialogue partners to help shape and sharpen its hermeneutical agenda of freedom from all oppression and of remaining critical, political, and relevant. It is my hope that African American

---

80. Herbert Robinson Marbury, *Pillars of Cloud and Fire: The Politics of Exodus in African American Biblical Interpretation* (New York: New York University Press, 2015).
81. Ibid., 8–9.
82. Emerson B. Powery and Rodney S. Sadler Jr., *The Genesis of Liberation: Biblical Interpretation in the Antebellum Narratives of the Enslaved* (Louisville: Westminster John Knox, 2016).

biblical interpretation will increasingly reflect the complexity of living and working as an African American in the African Diaspora and in dialogue with our sisters and brothers on the continent of Africa, as well as with other persons of color. Such complexity should include the intersectionality of race/ethnicity, class, gender, sexuality, age, nation/empire, (post/neo)coloniality, and dis/ability. It should also critically address the challenges and opposition that our transgendered sisters and brothers of color face while they attempt to live out their faith and callings but are finding few safe spaces in communities of faith. It is my hope that African American biblical scholars will continue to seek to connect with and engage as participants in grassroots justice-seeking movements like Black Lives Matters and allow such engagement to inform our interpretive endeavors; that we will find ways to embody justice-seeking so that we can truly speak from below and/or allow those on the ground to somehow be present in or speak through and in our work.

African American biblical interpretation would do well to continue to diversify the methodologies it employs. I hope it will continue to expand its conversation partners, critically drawing upon the historical and contemporary traditions, practices, artifacts, and ways of knowing of African and African American culture and lived experience. I hope we continue to blur and transgress the constructed boundaries of sacred and profane, including the one drawn between exegesis and eisegesis. We are always, all of us, reading *into* the text. The distinction between exegesis and eisegesis that the academy has constructed and that is demonstrated in much of our interpretive work is a somewhat superficial one. It betrays an unconscious or conscious adherence to Eurocentric mainstream scholarship's insistence that application, the demonstration of relevance, is still really marginal.

Additionally, African American biblical interpretation will continually develop as more and more African American biblical scholars emerge and engage in the task of interpretation, bringing their diverse concerns, interests, and methodological questions to the enterprise. I hope that African American men and women biblical scholars will seek to engage in more collaborative endeavors and create innovative spaces for critical conversations.

Womanist biblical interpretation, as a burgeoning contextual reading perspective prioritizing black women's voices, will continue to have a significant impact on biblical studies. Womanist biblical scholars might consider applying for a separate Womanist Biblical Interpretation Section within the Society of Biblical Literature (SBL) annual conference. Such a section would open up more space for critical engagement, collaboration, and mentorship, as well as an impetus for new creative works. I believe this could be an appropriate time to consider such a section, given the critical mass of womanist biblical scholars in the academy and the works they are producing.

Summary

In this chapter I have attempted to discuss the development and some significant contributions of African American and womanist biblical interpretation to the field of biblical studies in the twenty-first century. I have argued that race continues as the most significant social category of analysis, but not without intersecting with other social divisions like class, gender, and sexuality. African American and womanist biblical interpretation have always been interdisciplinary endeavors, using or engaging a plethora of methodologies and theories, but they are increasingly becoming more complex in their varied approaches to interpretation as a critical mass of women and men enter the field. To briefly summarize, in the twenty-first century African American biblical scholars have approached the task of interpretation to achieve the following:

- To create dialogue between African American lived experience and culture and biblical texts and contexts;

- To produce interpretations that have relevancy for Africana communities;

- To demonstrate the many ways that text and contexts can speak to and through African American experience;

- To demonstrate how African Americans have historically and critically read texts and contexts;

- To (re)construct and highlight images of blackness and identity in ancient texts and their function in those texts;

- To engage the complexity of black experience and identity by employing more complex intersectional analyses that considers race/ethnicity, gender, class, sexuality, and other mutually impacting and interconnected social categories to the task of interpretation;

- To engage in conversations with other diverse critical theories and voices, including postcolonial and critical race theories;

- To engage in corrective reconstruction and reimagining of texts and contexts in order to produce liberating interpretations and critical reflection;

- To honor the sacredness and legitimacy of black lived experiences, including revelation and knowledge production of African Americans pertaining to God and text and contexts;

- To decenter the biblical text while prioritizing African Americans and other peoples of color as readers.

4

Slavery, Torture, Systemic Oppression, and Kingdom Rhetoric: An African American Reading of Matthew 25:1–13

Oppressive structures are often adjusted to accommodate the changing fears and desires of the (neo)colonizers and/or dominant oppressors. The public face of an oppressive system can change (or alternate, at times), between oppressor and oppressed subordinated other; aspects of the new facade may even appear representative of the oppressed. But the death-dealing policies continue to the detriment of the oppressed. Oppressive systems must be exposed and deconstructed or dismantled (even in sacred texts), not simply recycled or cosmetically adjusted to palliate and opiate the oppressed and their allies. Studies have proven that black women and men, the poor, and other peoples of color are unfairly targeted by law enforcement; that they are more likely and disproportionately the victims of police profiling; that they receive longer prison terms for lesser crimes; that they are stereotyped as lazy, hypersexualized, and capable of more violence and criminal behavior than others; that they as a group make less money than their counterparts for doing the same jobs; and that, despite all this, they are expected to embrace a politics of respectability (an elitist ideology that requires them to quietly lift themselves up, acquiescing and gen-uflecting to unjust laws and practices, which results in victim blam-ing), even though justice eludes them and their rights are diminished.[1] Oppressive systems must be named, especially those structures that are embedded or reinscribed in sacred texts and contexts.

The biblical text sometimes lends itself to support oppressive struc-tures and disregard for human freedom and dignity in societies. A Gospel narrative, inclusive of slave parables replete with stereotypes, did not have to be perverted to support the inhumane system of slav-ery and its routine physical, spiritual, and psychological cruelties against African slaves. Matthew's Gospel, for example, abounds with slave parables in which exemplary stereotypical slave behavior serves as a model for persons desiring membership in the kingdom of heav-ens. Missionaries seeking to convert the black "soul" on southern American slave plantations recognized the usefulness of slave parables to help perpetuate slave ideology, making the connection between the "faithful slave" and the divine master. Palmer's *Plain and Easy Catechism* for slaves includes the following prayer: "Help me to be faithful to my owner's interest . . . may I never disappoint the trust that is placed in me, nor like the unjust steward, waste my master's goods."[2] For-mer slave Frederick Douglass recalled how Master Thomas would bind and for hours flog his crippled cousin Henny. After each brutal beat-ing Master Thomas would proclaim the following: "That servant which *knew his lord's will, and prepared not himself,* neither did according to his will, shall be beaten with many stripes"[3] (emphasis mine). It was inex-cusable for a slave to be ignorant of and/or fail to meet the master's demands, to be unprepared to fulfill his subordinate status as slave. If it

1. See Michelle Alexander, *The New Jim Crow: Incarceration in an Age of Color Blindness* (New York: New Press, 2012); Cheryl L. Neely, *You're Dead—So What? Media, Policy, and the Invisibility of Black Women as Victims of Homicide* (East Lansing: Michigan State University Press, 2015); Fredrick Harris and Robert Lieberman, *Beyond Discrimination: Racial Inequality in a Postracist Era* (New York: Russell Sage Foundation, 2013); and Kelly Brown Douglas, *Stand Your Ground: Black Bodies and the Justice of God* (Maryknoll, NY: Orbis, 2015).

2. Tammy K. Byron, "'A Catechism for Their Special Use': Slave Catechisms in the Antebellum South," PhD diss., University of Arkansas, 2008, 110–11. See Mitzi J. Smith, "U.S. Colonial Missions to African Slaves: Catechizing Black Souls, Traumatizing the Black *Psychē*," in *Teaching All Nations: Interrogating the Matthean Great Commission*, ed. Mitzi J. Smith and Lalitha Jayachitra (Minneapolis: Fortress Press, 2014), 57–85. See also Dave Gosse, "Examining the Promulgation and Impact of the Great Commission in the Caribbean, 1942–1970: A Historical Analysis," in Smith and Jayachitra, eds., *Teaching All Nations,* 33–56; Beatrice Okyere-Manu, "Colonial Mission and the Great Commis-sion in Africa, in Smith and Jayachitra, eds., *Teaching All Nations,* 15–32.

3. Frederick Douglass, *My Bondage and My Freedom,* 1855 Edition (New York: Dover Publications, 1969), 201.

was determined that a slave was negligent, most masters showed little mercy.

Unjust systems wreak havoc on the lives of the marginalized and the poor and make it possible to condone and justify their victimization. In the slave parables, slave ideology and brutality are reinscribed, sanitized, and sanctified with theological rhetoric. In Matthew 25:1-13 and its immediate context, the master–slave relationship, with its stereotypes, fears, and cruelties, functions as a legitimate metaphorical exemplar for participation in the kingdom of heavens. In this essay I read Matthew 25:1-13 through an African American interpretive lens that prioritizes black people's historical and contemporary experience with oppressive systems. My interpretive lens engages the slave testimony of former American slave Frederick Douglass's autobiography *My Bondage, My Freedom*; Page DuBois's examination of the etymology of the Greek word *basanos* and its development to refer to state sanctioned testing by torture in ancient texts; Homi Bhabha's postcolonial theory of "ambivalence" and the function of stereotypes; and Ange-Marie Hancock's social political theory of "a politics of disgust" that operated in the welfare reform debates under the Clinton Administration resulting in the passage of the Personal Responsibility Act in 1996, shifting blame onto victims. I shall argue that the ten virgins in the parable are stereotyped slaves, entrapped in an unjust, oppressive structure, who function as the potential collective bride of the bridegroom.

Re-Reading the Parable: Exposing Oppressive Structures

I read the parable of the ten virgins (Matt 25:1-13) in its literary context and as part of a trilogy of slave parables (the other two are about the faithful and wise slave overseer in 24:45-51, and the master's distribution of talents to his slaves in 25:14-30). In the parable of the ten virgins, which is peculiar to Matthew, Jesus likens the kingdom of the heavens to ten virgins (*parthenoi*) that go to meet the bridegroom. All the virgins take their lamps, but five are characterized as foolish (*mōrai*) for their failure to carry excess oil. The five wise (*phronimos*), having carried surplus oil for their lamps, are prepared for the groom's late arrival. The bridegroom delays (*chronizontos*) his appearance so long that all the virgins fall asleep. When all the sleeping virgins are awakened by the midnight alarm of the groom's arrival, the five foolish ones had burned through their oil. The five wise ones have oil reserves but seemingly insufficient to share with the five foolish. The wise virgins admonish their foolish sisters to buy their own oil. Once the foolish have gone shopping, the groom arrives. The overly prepared wise virgins arise, light their wicks, and resume as if they had not fallen asleep. With lighted lamps in the dead of night, the wise virgins greet their groom and enter into the final portion of the wedding festivities (*tous gamous*).[4] And the door is closed behind them. When the five foolish virgins return, requesting entrance, the master (*kurios*) rejects them: "I do not know you" (25:11, 12). At verse 13, the moral of the parable is given: "Stay awake, therefore, because you know neither the day nor the hour [of the master's arrival]."[5]

This parable, together with the slave parables that frame it, reinscribe oppressive structures, stereotypes, and tactics, including torture, particularly in the form of sleep deprivation. Tortured submissive slaves are presented as exemplary participants/members of the eschatological kingdom of the heavens, and God is likened to a harsh slavemaster. When God is represented as a patriarchal enslaver in Scripture, many readers are reluctant or will not permit themselves to critique the harmful stereotypes and unjust systemic demands inscribed in the text, or the oppressive depictions of God. Further, I propose that the kingdom rhetoric itself is very problematic.

Absentee Bride or Slave Brides?

Most interpreters have resigned themselves to the conclusion that the bride is absent from the Matthew's wedding parable in chapter 25.[6] Amy-Jill Levine asserts that the ten virgins are "more likely, servants waiting for the groom to return to his home."[7] I propose that the ten virgins are all potential or intended brides of the one groom and not, euphemistically speaking, servants, but, rather, slave brides. Several ancient interpreters from the early third century through the early fifth century CE arrived at this same hermeneutical position: the virgins are brides. Hippolytus of Rome (170–235 CE) in an allegorical inter-

---

4. The use of the plural form of the Greek word *gamos* (wedding) at Matthew 25:10 likely indicates that the wedding celebration had several components. The plural *gamos* is also used in Matthew 22:1–10 (cf. Luke 14:16–24), which is the story of the king who gave a wedding celebration (*gamous*) for his son and dispatched invitations by way of his slaves.

5. All Scripture translations are mine unless otherwise noted.

6. For example, Amy-Jill Levine, "Gospel of Matthew," in *The Women's Bible Commentary: Twentieth-Anniversary Edition, Revised and Updated*, ed. Carol A. Newsom, Sharon H. Ringe, and Jacqueline E. Lapsley (Louisville: Westminster John Knox, 2012), 465–77, at 476.

7. Ibid.

pretation of the ten virgins in Matthew 25 wrote the following: "come, ye maidens, who desired my bride-chamber, and loved no other bride-groom than me, who by your testimony and habit of life were wedded to me, the immortal and incorruptible Bridegroom . . . come all, inherit the kingdom prepared for you from the foundation of the world."[8] Methodius—also known as Euboulios, Bishop of Olympus, and Patara in Lycia (260–312 CE)—in his only complete extant work, titled *Banquet of the Ten Virgins* (or *Concerning Chastity*), praises the virginal life, in both men and women. He, too, produced an allegorical interpretation of the Matthean parable of the ten virgins, writing that those who preserve their virginity are "being brought as a bride to the son of God." The number ten is symbolic of those who believe in Jesus Christ and have taken the "only right way to heaven." Five also here refers to five senses or "pathways of virtue—sight, taste, smell, touch, and hearing." Methodius further states that those who have maintained their virginity are "all under the one name of His spouse; for the spouse must be betrothed to the Bridegroom."[9] Finally, St. Augustine of Hippo (354–430 CE) also reads the parable allegorically. Similar to Methodius he understands the five and five (ten virgins) as representative of five senses. Augustine asserts that the wise virgins represent those having good works in the catholic church of God. Together the five represent the church, or the bride, that is espoused to "one husband."[10]

I imagine that the virgins had completed their nuptials and were journeying to the groom's residence to consummate the marriage, the final stage of the ceremonies.[11] Significantly, the Greek word *gamos* (wedding) appears only late in the parable when the groom arrives and enters into the *gamos* with "the prepared women" or wise virgins (25:10). Also, the parable as extended metaphor need not signify a contemporary first-century CE social practice or ideal, but it could reference knowledge of a shared cultural past. When Rome and other ancient slave societies (and some not considered slave societies, like

---

8. Hippolytus of Rome, "Appendix to his works. Containing dubious and spurious pieces," XLII, 53, *Ante-Nicene Fathers, Appendix*, vol. 5, ed. Alexander Roberts and James Donaldson (Peabody, MA: Hendrickson, 1995), 252–53.

9. Methodius, *Banquet of the Ten Virgins*, "The Parable of the Virgins," Discourse VI, Chapter III, 330; Discourse VII, Chapter I, 331.

10. St. Augustine of Hippo, *The Works of St. Augustine*, Sermon XLIII: 1–3, 15, *Nicene and Post-Nicene Fathers*, vol. 6: *Augustine: Sermon on the Mount, Harmony of the Gospels, Homilies on the Gospels*, ed. Philip Schaff (Peabody, MA: Hendrickson, 2004), 402.

11. Anthony Everitt, *Cicero: The Life and Times of Rome's Greatest Politician* (New York: Random House, 2003). When Cicero married in 79 BCE, after the wedding ceremony, the bride journeyed to her bridal home to meet her new husband and to consummate the marriage, preceded by a little girl carrying a torch. This elaborate ceremony was generally eliminated after the late Republic.

Israel) conquered other nations, they often enslaved the most useful human plunder. Some situations resulted in the taking of female virgins forcing them to become wives to their captors. For example, in Judges 21:12–23 the tribes of Israel conquered Jabesh-Gilead and enslaved four hundred young virgins, giving them to the Benjaminites as wives. When additional virgins were needed, Israel plundered virgins from Shiloh. According to legend, Romulus (Rome's first king) and his men, seeking an alliance with Sabine, took at least thirty Sabine virgins as wives.[12] Among the most important uses for slaves were sexual and marital functions.[13] I propose that the social practice or ideal the parable references is the wedding festivities of virginal female slaves, forming a Matthean slave trilogy; it is sandwiched between two other slave parables. The female slaves were given to a king or some other powerful figure as potential brides/wives; this fits well with the emphasis on kingdom. The king was the ultimate master; he could take as many wives as he pleased, when he pleased. Contrary to what Jennifer Glancy asserts in her book *Slavery in the Early Church*, Luke 12:42–48 is not the only parable to mention female slaves.[14]

In the trilogy of slave parables, Matthew's Jesus reads master–slave relations through the lens of a divine or sacralized kingdom rhetoric. Sacralized kingdom rhetoric sanitizes and obscures the oppressive power dynamics inherent in the master–slave ideology signified in the parable. The cruel master–slave relationship is idealized and presented as exemplary. And depictions of stereotypical master–slave relations become foundational and a component of iconic kingdom rhetoric, creating an unholy alliance.

Fear, Fetish, and Stereotypes: Putative Truths and Ambivalence

Virginity as a social construct carries its own stereotypes (e.g., virgins are modest, prudes, absolutely submissive, girlish, morally superior). The social construction of women as virgins is grounded in male fear and desire, or what Homi Bhabha calls phobia and fetish. In the labeling of some virgins as "foolish" and others as "wise," the fear/phobia and desire/fetish dichotomy emerges. Masters and oppressive systems desire wise virgins, but wise in their unwavering submission to the sys-

12. Plutarch, "Life of Romulus," in *Parallel Lives*, trans. Bernadotte Perrin, Loeb Classical Library 1 (Cambridge: Harvard University Press, 1914), 29–31.
13. Orlando Patterson, *Slavery and Social Death: A Comparative Study* (Cambridge: Harvard University Press, 1982), 173.
14. Jennifer A. Glancy, *Slavery in the Early Church* (Minneapolis: Fortress Press, 2006), 111.

tem, regardless of circumstance. Foolish virgins are feared because the system cannot control them. Their presence is a threat to the system and the authority of their masters. Bhabha argues that "there is both a structural and functional justification for reading the racial stereotype of colonial discourse in terms of fetishism. . . . The fetish or stereotype gives access to an 'identity' which is predicated as much on mastery and pleasure as it is on anxiety and defence, for it is a form of multiple and contradictory belief in its recognition of difference and disavowal of it."[15] Female slaves in the parable of the ten virgins reflect the stereotype that conceives slaves as inherently lazy, evil, worthless, and foolish (unless compelled to act other*wisely*). Such stereotypical behaviors are confirmed when half of the virgins fail to conform to the system/master's expectations, regardless of how capricious and unjust. Simultaneously and somewhat contradictorily, when slaves do not conform to the system's expectations it is because they are considered naturally inferior. People are either innately slaves or masters, as Aristotle argued. Good and wise slaves are loyal, industrious, useful, and constantly and consciously available or *awake*. An embedded social structure built upon these stereotypes transverses the trilogy of slave parables. Oppressive systems and structures employ stereotypes.

Yet, as Bhabha also asserts, it is insufficient to focus on negative or positive images; we must shift to the *"processes of subjectification"* that stereotypes make possible.[16] We should consider how the stereotype effectively functions. The stereotype functions through *ambivalence*, by stating what is supposedly fact and putative truth *and* also by demonstrating the need to anxiously repeat what is supposedly already known and needing no proof. The stereotype as the major discursive strategy of the discourse of colonialism "is a form of knowledge and identification that vacillates between what is always 'in place,' already known, and something that must be anxiously repeated . . . as if the essential duplicity of the Asiatic or the bestial sexual license of the African that needs no proof, can never really, in discourse, be proved."[17] This process of *ambivalence* is central to the stereotype. I argue that the placement of the three slave parables together in Matthew accomplishes a repetition and a reification of the stereotype across the parables. The stereotypical characterization of the wise and

15. Homi K. Bhabha, "The Other Question: Stereotype, Discrimination and the Discourse of Colonialism," in *The Location of Culture*, ed. Homi K. Bhabha (New York: Routledge, 1994), 94–120, at 106, 107.
16. Ibid., 95.
17. Ibid.

foolish virginal slave women stands in continuity with the stereotypical slaves characterized in the other two parables in the trilogy.

The trilogy (ten virginal female slaves; the faithful [*pistos*] and wise [*phronimos*] slave overseer; and the slaves entrusted with their master's money) illustrates Jesus's admonishment to "stay awake" (*grēgoreō*), which is necessary because of the uncertainty of the parousia (future coming of the Son of Man) (24:36–44). This same warning summarizes the second parable's meaning (25:13). Several themes found in the Matthean Jesus's instruction about the parousia are repeated in the slave trilogy: lack of knowledge about the parousia, the unexpected arrival, marriage, careless and wasteful behavior, watchfulness, staying awake, ownership, and preparedness. Also, we notice a focus on division and duality: half are taken/received or commended (the good/wise/prepared/working/awake) and half are left, reprimanded, or disposed of (the wicked/foolish/unprepared/idle/sleeping).

In the parable of the ten virgins, the wise virgins are expected to be prepared for the bridegroom's arrival with constantly burning lamps in order to consummate the marriage. Similarly, in the parable of the wise overseer, when the master arrives, he should discover the slave working. In that parable, time is also an issue. In the master's absence the wise overseer is expected to give the master's other slaves their food allowance at the proper time (*en kairō*). The master's delay should not disrupt the expectations that masters have of their slaves and slaves of their masters: a good slave always behaves as if the master sees and knows everything. Conversely, the wicked overseer wastes time in eating and drinking; and, behaving like a cruel slavemaster, he abuses his fellow slaves (24:48–49). Stereotypically, a slave will behave like a master and become the abuser when afforded the opportunity. When the slave overseer shifts from abused to abuser in the master's absence, he is depicted as conforming "to the cultural expectation of ancient audiences."[18]

Knowing that all slaves are potentially "wicked" or "good," the master will arrive at an unexpected time to catch them off guard (24:50). Masters can pronounce slaves as either good or wicked, oscillating between the two, depending on their willingness and ability to respond to the master's every (and ever-changing) whim. The wicked slave will be mutilated and cast among the hypocrites where there will be "weeping and gnashing of teeth" (24:51). "No slave society took the position

18. J. Albert Harrill, "The Psychology of Slaves in the Gospel Parables: A Case Study in Social History," *Biblische Zeitschrift* 55 (2011): 63–74, at 73.

that the slave, being a thing, would not be held responsible for his actions,"[19] or failure to act.

In the third parable in the trilogy, similar to the parable of the wise overseer, the soon-to-be-absent master entrusts his slaves with his property (25:14-30). The master's property consists of all he owns, including the slave's body/sexuality, time, labor, and peculium.[20] The master gives each slave a specific amount of money/talents. Each slave increases the master's money except the one who received one talent. That slave confesses that his master is harsh and engages in unsavory business practices. Thus, acting from fear, he chooses to bury the one talent, rather than risk losing it and suffering the cruel consequences. The master left no instructions that each slave should increase his money; that was an unspoken expectation between master and slave. Slaves are expected always to fear their masters. But that fear should compel them always to act to further the master's economic interests. The slave with one talent was expected to do exactly what the master would have done: reap where he did not plant. After much time the master returns and rewards the two slaves who increased his holdings with greater responsibilities (more work and less rest!). The slaves that met or exceeded the master's expectations continue in the master-slave relationship. But the wicked, lazy and worthless slave is punished. Like, the wicked slave overseer in the first parable (24:49-50), this wicked slave will also be cast into outer darkness (25:30). The "wicked" slaves are rendered total outcasts (beyond social death) to be forever subject to torture: "there shall be weeping and gnashing of teeth" (Matt 8:12; 22:13; 24:51; 25:30; Luke 13:28). A slave never escapes torture or the stigmatization of her being.

The most prominent dimension of Matthew's representation of slavery is "the slave's body as the locus of abuse."[21] The abuse may be more evident in the case of the first and third slave parables than in the parable of the ten virgins. I propose that the abuse against the slaves' bodies, including the foolish virgins, is also manifested in the expectation (and failure) of the slaves to make their bodies and labor constantly available to the master. The virgins are expected to stay awake until the groom arrives, no matter how long his delay and how

---

19. Patterson, *Slavery and Social Death*, 196.
20. Peculium was property and assets that masters placed at the slave's disposal, such as cash, land, clothing, or other slaves. Slaves could not own property; the peculium legally belonged to the master. A. F. Rodger, "Peculium," in *The Oxford Classical Dictionary*, 3d ed., ed. S. Hornblower and A. Spawforth (New York: Oxford University Press, 1996), 110.
21. Glancy, *Slavery in the Early Church*, 113.

tired they may become. And in their fatigue, they are expected to consummate the marriage. Slave bodies should be perpetually available to the groom/master's desires. The master's capricious refusal to let the five foolish virgins participate in the final festivities constitutes their rejection as wives; virgins are good for nothing if not to become wives.[22] Their rejection is their "weeping and gnashing of teeth" experience. When virgins taken from conquered peoples are rejected, they are subject to further social isolation or physical death—"slavery is the . . . violent domination of naturally alienated and generally dishonored persons."[23] That which saved them from physical death—their virginity—is rejected.

By their failure to overly prepare for the master/groom's capricious delay, the five foolish virgins fail to manifest in their bodies the truth of their availability to the master's unmitigated desires; it is a failure to bring the truth into the light, to make it known, recognizable. Masters determine what is knowable, recognizable, or legitimate. The neglect exhibited by the five foolish virgins (insufficient oil) maybe understood as "forgetting." The Greek noun *alētheia* (truth) bears some connection with the idea of "something not forgotten, not slipping by unnoticed."[24] Forgetting is to leave knowledge hidden, a failure to uncover truth, to bring it to a point of utility or usefulness.

In summary, the three parables share a stereotypical characterization of slaves and slavery as a system of oppression: Slaves are expected to respond to their master's whims; to demonstrate unwavering loyalty to their masters; to be "wise," but only with regard to fulfilling their slave duties and not foolish in falling short of expectations; to expect cruelty from their masters, especially when they fail to perform; to be dispensable if they do not perform in ways that furthers the master's economic interests and physical desires; and to be concerned only with pleasing the master. Good and wise slaves do not challenge the system or their servitude. The kingdom of heaven is revealed in the loyalty, vigilance, and wakefulness of slaves, but it is also grounded in difference—differences among slaves as well as between slaves and masters.

22. See Mary F. Foskett, *A Virgin Conceived: Mary and Classical Representations of Virginity* (Bloomington: Indiana University Press, 2002), 44–55.
23. Patterson, *Slavery and Social Death*, 13. Patterson offers a comparative analysis of slavery based on 66 of the 186 slaveholding societies listed by George Murdock's sample of world societies.
24. Page DuBois, *Torture and Truth: The New Ancient World* (New York/London: Routledge, 1991), 84, 85.

Stay Awake! Sleep Deprivation as Torture and Extracting Truth

In contemporary American society, where we are experiencing an epidemic of police brutality against black and brown bodies, the United Nations' Human Rights Council has officially recognized this epidemic of racism and police violence against minorities as a human rights violation.[25] In America, the burden is once again placed on the backs of African Americans and other people of color to avoid violent police interactions by conducting themselves in certain "respectable" ways. Not only are people of color as victims of biased policing and police brutality under assault from outside of their communities, but also from some elite members of their own communities, who blame them for their victimization on account of their failure to practice "respectability politics." But as history and contemporary events have demonstrated, "respectability politics" will not save one's life when systems and structures remain oppressive and unjust. African Americans and other people of color are to increase their vigilance, taking care never to arouse the suspicion or fears of police officers or neighborhood-watch people (primarily white) in the manner of Trayvon Martin or Keith Lamont Scott, both of whom are, of course, dead. African Americans must stay 'woke, always answerable to a "respectability politics" that requires black people never to express an attitude, move too fast, openly carry guns with a permit in open-carry states, change lanes without signaling, or walk or run away from a police officer, lest they meet an untimely and brutal death at the hands of authority figures for whom the same wakefulness and prudence is not always required.

As the slave parables in biblical texts demonstrate, slaves should never oversleep or fall asleep when they are expected to be awake and working in a way that displays their subordinate status (cf. Mark 13:34–35). The slave body was unable to rest at night.[26] Seneca, on the mistreatment of slaves, states that a slave whose duty it was to serve wine was forced to "dress like a woman" and compelled to "remain awake throughout the night, dividing his time between his master's

---

25. Natasja Sheriff, "US cited for police violence, racism in scathing UN review on human rights," Aljazeera America, May 11, 2015, http://america.aljazeera.com/articles/2015/5/11/us-faces-scathing-un-review-on-human-rights-record.html.
26. Glancy, *Slavery in Early Christianity*, 105.

drunkenness and his lust."[27] Some slaves were ordered to serve food all night "hungry and dumb."[28]

Similarly, African slaves in America were expected to work from sunup to sundown—"the night is shortened on both ends."[29] Frederick Douglass wrote that "more slaves are whipped for oversleeping than for any other fault."[30] Slaves were not afforded regular beds but were given "one coarse blanket" on which to sleep. The greatest problem was not the lack of a proper bed, however, but the "want of time to sleep," since the present day's field work and preparation for the following day's labor consumed most of their sleeping hours, leaving little time to care for their own domestic needs like washing and cooking.[31]

Slavery itself and the pervasive cruelty to which slaves were subjected, as stereotypically inscribed in the slave parables, in ancient slave societies, and in American slavery, was torture. Similar to how slaves in antiquity were tortured to extract truth from their bodies in disputes between masters, African American slaves were "sometimes whipped into the confession of offenses which [they] never committed"; on plantations slaves were not considered innocent until proven guilty (the same can be said of many African Americans murdered in this twenty-first century by police officers).[32] In ancient slave societies "[t]he *basanos* [testing by torture] assumes first that the slave always lies, then that torture makes him or her always tell the truth, then that the truth produced through torture will always expose the truth or falsehood of the free man's evidence."[33] Regarding American slavery, Douglass writes that "[s]uspicion and torture are the approved methods of getting at the truth. . . . It was necessary for me, therefore, *to keep a watch* over my deportment, less the enemy should get the better of me."[34] More specifically, sleep deprivation routinely imposed upon slaves or required on particular occasions to meet the master's special needs should also be viewed as torture.

27. Seneca, *Ad Lucilum Epistulae Morales*, trans. J. W. Basore, Loeb Classical Library 47 (Cambridge: Harvard University Press, 1979), 7, 8.
28. Ibid., 3.
29. Douglass, *My Bondage*, 102.
30. Ibid.
31. Frederick Douglass, *Narrative of the Life of Frederick Douglass, an American Slave, Written by Himself* (Boston, 1845), in *Slave Narratives*, ed. William L. Andrews and Henry Louis Gates Jr. (New York: Library of America, 2000), 267–368, at 287.
32. Ibid., 277.
33. DuBois, *Torture and Truth*, 36. *Basanos* evolves from a literal meaning of "touchstone" to a metaphorized sense of a test and then returns to a concrete meaning of actual physical testing of a slave's body by torture.
34. Douglass, *My Bondage*, 277–78 (emphasis mine).

Wise slaves stay awake to serve their masters; good slaves are constantly available to masters. Wicked/foolish slaves fail to stay awake *and* are unprepared to meet the master's needs; they are denied participation and/or "citizenship" in the kingdom of the heavens. Douglass writes that "[t]he good slave must be whipped, to be *kept* good, and the bad slave must be whipped, to be *made* good."[35] A society based on slave–master hierarchy requires torture to produce good slaves and control wicked ones. Viewed through the slave parables, the kingdom of the heavens, like the ancient *polis*, maintains a social hierarchy of slave and free. DuBois asserts that torture in ancient Athenian society, "[i]n the work of the wheel, the rack, and the whip, the torturer carries out the work of the polis; citizen is made distinct from noncitizen, Greek from barbarian, slave from free."[36] DuBois omits sleep deprivation as a form of state-sanctioned torture. I propose that sleep deprivation is both integral to torture of any kind and constitutes torture in its own right.

The effective extracting of "truthful" testimony through torture relies on the consciousness of the slave. A slave must be awake for torture to be operative. Inherent to all torture is sleep deprivation—a sleeping slave is not, cannot be, a tortured slave; he cannot feel pain and give testimony to truths when sleeping. A truth that is inscribed in the slave's body daily is the truth of his inferiority and the master's superiority. How is the "truth" of the slave's inferiority inscribed in his body and then extracted? Truth is both inscribed and extracted from the slave's body by his submissive obedience, especially in the master's absence, and through acts of torture, such as sleep deprivation, beatings, crucifixion/lynching, withholding of food, and dangling before her promises of liberties that freeborn persons enjoy. The Matthean slave trilogy uses staying awake as a test of loyal slaves who in their submission embody truth about the kingdom of the heavens; it demands wakefulness. Sleep deprivation and other forms of mundane cruelties like whipping constituted the American slave plantation as judicial space where slavery and slaves were always on trial. The slave's body daily endures systematic torture/punishment as a sort of truth telling.

The ancients did not seem to make a distinction between torture and punishment when it came to slaves,[37] but in certain spaces torture

---

35. Ibid., 258–59.
36. DuBois, *Torture and Truth*, 63.
37. For example, on p. 55 of *Torture and Truth*, DuBois inserts a quote of the last speech from

or punishment of slaves was communally authorized and codified for the purpose of settling disputes between masters requiring slave testimony. The ability of slaves to function satisfactorily despite and because of abuse (e.g., sleep deprivation) served as a testimony to the slave's suitability for slavery. DuBois asserts that "the slave, incapable of reasoning, can only produce truth under coercion, can produce only truth under coercion. . . . Proof, and therefore, truth, are constituted by the Greeks as best found in the evidence derived from torture. Truth, *alêtheia*, comes from elsewhere, from another place, from the place of the other."[38]

In the slave trilogy a connection is made between wisdom and staying awake/sleep deprivation: wise and faithful slaves will be awake when the master arrives. All slaves entrusted with the master's property and money should have remained vigilant regarding the master's expectations. The ten virginal slaves should not have fallen asleep waiting for the master's arrival. The overpreparedness of the five wise virginal slaves saved them, despite the fact that they, too, fell asleep. They at least gave an appearance of being continually awake and vigilant; they jumped up from their sleep to trim and light their lamps as if their lamps had never gone out. It would have been hazardous to their health had the ten virgins fallen asleep and left their lamps burning. Regardless of the lateness of the hour, the virginal brides were to be prepared to consummate the marriage. Such physical sacrifice made them wise. A slave who continues with her duties despite sleep deprivation—torture—is of superior value, is considered faithful, and can enter into the master's bridal chamber and be known by him. Manifested in the wise submissive slave's body is the truth of the master's total domination over her.

To torture a slave as a witness is a means of extracting truth from a body deemed otherwise unable or unwilling to proffer truth. There is only distortion or absence of truth when slaves fail to meet the system's demands and the master's expectations. Slaves that carry in their sleep-deprived bodies the truth of their subordination are considered wise. Wisdom is associated with truthfulness in the biblical text.[39] Five of the virgins were wise because they rendered the necessary and

Antiphon's First Tetralogy (ii, d, 7), which partially reads "whereas this slave, who gave us no opportunity of either cross-examining or torturing him—when can he be punished? No, when can he be cross-examined?" Also see *Torture and* Truth, 38.

38. DuBois, *Torture and Truth*, 68.
39. Celia Deutsch, "Wisdom in Matthew: Transformation of a Symbol," *Novum Testamentum* 32 (1990): 13–47, at 17.

ostensibly uninterrupted service to the groom/master despite falling asleep.

Wisdom and a Gendered Apartheid

Kimberly Russaw argues that "prevailing scholarly treatments of Wisdom Literature rarely ascribe wisdom to female characters. Wisdom is personified as feminine in Proverbs, but biblical scholars rarely argue for women as the beneficiaries of wisdom and [such] scholarly treatments of wisdom are overwhelmingly male-centered."[40] Even the wisdom of the ten virgins is androcentric; they are wise in relation to the slavemaster/groom's expectations. "Like the slave body that needs the supplement of the *basanos* [testing of the body through torture] to produce truth, the female body and the fragmentary text are both constructed as lacking."[41] Both lack the capacity for loyalty and truth until they demonstrate loyalty and truth, how and when the master demands. The five wise virgins show their wisdom by anticipating and adjusting their behavior to meet the demands of an unjust playing field, which compels them to be overprepared and less than generous toward their sisters. According to Russaw, a wise woman is skillful and crafty, possesses the ability to see things (not necessarily in foretelling the future), and pursues what she understands to be good.[42] The five wise virgins demonstrate skill and craftiness (cf. 10:16) and servile foresight in expecting the master's delay.

The only other wise female in Matthew is Lady Wisdom (*hē sophia*), justified by her deeds (11:19; cf. 11:25, 23:34; Luke 7:35), but who is masculinized in the person of Jesus who "assumes Wisdom's roles,"[43] especially by the performance of powerful deeds (11:19–20). Matthew redacts his sources to show that Jesus is not "primus inter pares [first among equals] among Wisdom's messengers, but rather to be identified with personified Wisdom itself."[44] The five wise virgins remain the only women in Matthew labeled as wise. But their wisdom is not *sophia* wisdom, but *phronimos* or intelligence circumscribed and mollified by their status as enslaved virgins. Not even the Virgin Mary is described as

40. Kimberly D. Russaw, "Wisdom in the Garden: The Woman of Genesis 3 and Alice Walker's *Sophia*," in *I Found God in Me: A Womanist Biblical Hermeneutics Reader*, ed. Mitzi J. Smith (Eugene, OR: Cascade, 2015), 222–34, at 226. See Elisabeth Schüssler Fiorenza, *Jesus: Miriam's Child, Sophia's Prophet: Critical Issues in Feminist Christology* (New York: Continuum, 1995).
41. DuBois, *Torture and Truth*, 95.
42. Russaw, "Wisdom in the Garden," 227–29.
43. Levine, "Gospel of Matthew," 472.
44. Deutsch, "Wisdom in Matthew," 35.

wise in Matthew (cf. Luke 1:48, the Virgin Mary is a lowly slave [doulē]. Yet, the male child that she births is "filled with wisdom [sophia]," Luke 2:40). Slaves are not innately good or wise (sophos), but they are wise (phronimos) in relation to other slaves, reinforcing the stereotype of the slave as inherently foolish, lazy, and/or wicked.[45] Truth/wisdom must be extracted from slaves; they need masters who torture them. In the Synoptics the Greek noun phronimos occurs only in parables or parabolic sayings and "applies to those who have grasped the eschatological position" of human beings.[46] Thus, in the slave parables the word is applied to those slaves who accept and demonstrate their subordination, which transcends the eschatological parousia. In God's eschatological judgment, slaves remain slaves.

Just as some slaves are considered wicked/lazy or faithful/wise, the rhetorical division of women as wise and foolish can be viewed as a gendered apartheid. Matthew favors this division. The Q material at Matthew 7:24-25 is the parable of the wise (phronimos) and foolish (mōros) men who build houses on rock and sand, respectively (Luke's version, 6:47-49, does not characterize the men as wise or foolish). The man who builds his house on the sand is wise in relation to another man and with respect to building a house with the proper foundation. Similarly, as I have shown, the wise virgins are wise in relation to other virgins and with respect to being presciently prepared for the groom's late arrival. The wise virgins are not the same as the Proverbs 31 woman who is described as wise and virtuous. Slave women can be virgins but not virtuous. The Proverbs 31 woman is an elite, free woman of means. She owns slaves, providing food for her household and duties for her slave girls. She can buy fields and hardly ever goes out at night; she can afford to give to the poor and needy. But the five wise virgins cannot afford to share with their sisters in their hour of need; all are slaves and therefore not encouraged to act communally within a system of apartheid. Dividing people within oppressed groups, giving them a false sense of superiority over their sisters and brothers, is characteristic of racial and gender oppression. If oppressors can convince the oppressed that the noncompliant behavior of their brothers and sisters to systemic oppression is the cause of their suffering, then the system itself is rendered innocuous and truthful.

---

45. See Peter Garnsey, *Ideas of Slavery from Aristotle to Augustine* (Cambridge: Cambridge University Press, 1996), 74.
46. Georg Betram, "*phronimos*," *Theological Dictionary of the New Testament*, 10th ed., ed. Gerhard Kittel and Gerhard Friedrich (Grand Rapids: Eerdmans, 1984), 9:234.

If the broader public and policymakers can be convinced of the truthfulness of a stereotype, creating a disgust for those who are stereotyped, then the stereotype becomes effective. Thus, readers automatically accept the designation of five virgins as foolish condoning their fate and ultimate rejection. Ange-Marie Hancock says that a "politics of disgust" preserves the hegemony of the stereotype, creating/maintaining a context of inequality by silencing the voices of the oppressed and destroying any political solidarity between elite classes and the oppressed. Such was the case in the 1996 policy debates around welfare reform that resulted in biased and unjust policies based on the myth of the welfare queen. Elite sisters of all races abandoned poor black women whom President Reagan had dubbed, and falsely so, the face of the so-called welfare queens. Microlevel personal or individual explanations are employed to the exclusion of systemic explanations.[47] As Emilie Townes notes, that welfare queen construct is a modern version of the black matriarch; they fail to model "good" gender conduct, refusing to be passive, which "leads to the stigmatization of Black women who insist on controlling their sexuality and fertility."[48] Further, as Townes argues, such stigmatized black women "do not serve the interests of the classist, racist, and sexist social order of the fantastic hegemonic imagination."[49] The "fantastic hegemonic imagination traffics in peoples' lives that are caricatured or pillaged so that the imagination that creates the fantastic can control the world in its own image."[50] Each parable in the trilogy reinscribes master–slave caricatures through which the author hopes to promote and/or discourage certain behaviors. Certain submissive behaviors are promoted as worthy of participation in the kingdom; such behaviors encourage and reward individualism and classism within an oppressive system that serves as a vision for kingdom relations. Slaves who stay awake at all costs, submitting to the extraction of the truth of their subordination from their bodies, exemplify those who can participate in the kingdom of the heavens. In the parables, slave–master ideology is used to construct, describe (and for some prescribes), sacralize and normalize violent and abusive behaviors, subordinated and stereotypical relationships, and cruel and unfair expectations for God and for those who

47. Ange-Marie Hancock, *The Politics of Disgust* (New York: New York University Press, 2004), 25.
48. Emilie M. Townes, *Womanist Ethics and the Cultural Production of Evil* (New York: Palgrave Macmillan, 2006), 117.
49. Ibid.
50. Ibid., 21.

wish to participate in the kingdom of the heavens, as realized on earth and as anticipated in the future.

Slavery and Kingdom Rhetoric

Like Luke's Gospel, Matthew contains more slave parables than Mark or John.[51] The Matthean Jesus's use of parables comparing the kingdom of the heavens to the stereotypical interactions between masters and slaves is tantamount to conforming the gospel and the character of God/Jesus to the master–slave paradigm, rather than transforming relationships and oppressive systems into the likeness of a loving, compassionate God. By systematically framing slave parables in kingdom-of-the-heavens language, the author of Matthew mollifies and normalizes the cruelty of slavery, sanctifies the language that signifies the oppression, and makes it difficult for (neo)colonized, oppressed, and/or marginalized "people of the book" to fully name, reject, and heal from oppression and oppressive systems. What might have been the psychological and social impact of these slave parables and their kingdom rhetoric on first-century believers, many of whom might have been slaves themselves? The Jesus movement appealed to slave and free, master and slave, noble persons and peasants.[52] The social reality of systemic oppression signified by slave parables baptized in kingdom-of-the-heavens rhetoric promotes stereotypical slave behavior and oppressive relationships as ideals worthy of imitation and transcending time and space. Also, such parables, including the parable of the ten virginal slave brides, reinscribe stereotypes that justify the subordination of certain peoples and systems of hierarchical oppression.

Further, our trilogy of slave parables and similar parables used to teach about the nature of the kingdom of the heavens/God and its participants continue to reinforce the longstanding marriage of kingdom building, slavery, and religion/theologies. Slavery is a function of nation and empire building and maintenance; historically, empires conquer and enslave. Slavery is an inherent and putative aspect of kingdom/nation building providing a reservoir of free human labor compelled to work day and night. This fact raises the question of the appropriateness of "kingdom" language as a metaphor or descriptor

51. According to Glancy, "[no] trajectory of the Jesus tradition lacks slave sayings"; *Slavery in the Early Church*, 107.
52. Patterson asserts that "It is generally accepted that Christianity found many of its earliest converts among the slave populations of the Roman Empire, although the fact is surprisingly difficult to authenticate"; *Slavery and Social Death*, 70.

for a justice- and love-oriented community. According to 1 Samuel 8:10–18, God warned Israel against replicating kingdom building because their sons would be conscripted, their land, labor, and slaves confiscated, and the people would become slaves of the king. Slavery is understood to be a putative reality of kingdom building/maintenance. But it is preferable to own slaves than to become a slave; to be the victor rather than the victim; the oppressor and not the oppressed. When oppressive structures are not dismantled but are occupied by even well-meaning folks and replicated, some *will be* oppressors and others *will be* oppressed.

Matthew inundates his readers with kingdom imagery and language. In Matthew's genealogy Jesus is the Messiah through the Davidic royal dynasty (1:1, 16–18, 20). As one of the most famous and beloved kings in Israelite history, David's dynasty would be perpetual, so said the Deuteronomistic writers (2 Sam 2:7). In Jesus the kingdom of the heavens had come near. John the Baptist, Jesus, and his disciples preached the good news of the kingdom of the heavens (3:2; 4:17; 10:7). In Matthew alone, Jesus is called the "king of the Jews" toward the beginning of the Gospel in the same narrative context that introduces King Herod (2:1). Herod, the puppet king and extension of the Roman Empire, fears that the baby Jesus is the rumored "king of the Jews" who might grow up to usurp his place. The kingdom rhetoric and the significant and numerous presentations of servile slave behavior and good master–slave relations as exemplars demonstrate that Matthew is not a "counternarrative" or "work of resistance," as Warren Carter once argued. Nor does Matthew position himself or speak against the status quo of Roman hegemonic imperial power,[53] at least not consistently or without contradictions. Matthew does not seek to change the system, just the face of those occupying positions of authority within the system. Filling the same old oppressive structures with different people is deceptive; a new driver does not a new chariot/car make. Carter has argued that reading and hearing Matthew as counternarrative "unveils and resists a center that comprises the powerful political and religious elite."[54] More recently, Carter has concluded that Matthew both critiques and imitates Roman imperial practices and ideas;[55] Fernando Segovia states that Carter reads Matthew

53. Warren Carter, *Matthew and the Margins: A Socio-Political and Religious Reading* (Sheffield, UK: Sheffield University Press, 2000), 1.
54. Ibid., 3.
55. Warren Carter, "The Gospel of Matthew," in *A Postcolonial Commentary of the New Testament Writings*,

as a "conflicted text,"[56] which may be a more accurate characterization. It seems that Matthew too often, particularly with his use of slave parables, speaks from and stands in the center of the status quo. The colonized sometimes unwittingly internalize their own oppression. As Musa Dube argues, the Matthean community is not subversive to Roman imperialism; Matthew is a postcolonial text, written by the subjugated, that certifies imperialism,[57] if unwittingly. I wonder whether Matthew could have been a slaveholder like Philemon. Perhaps Matthew was a wealthy slaveholder who was as prosperous as the "relatively wealthy urban community" reflected in his Gospel.[58] Or maybe Matthew was neither a slaveholder nor a wealthy person, but simply a victim of colonization who unintentionally coopted his own oppression by inscribing slavery and kingdom-of-the-heavens rhetoric in his text. Readers accept the union of kingdom rhetoric and slavery as holy and sanctified because it is inscribed in their sacred and authoritative text. "What God has joined together [religion, slavery/oppression and kingdom building], let no human being separate" (Mark 9:10).

Few kingdoms, nations or empires have been built without the use of slave labor.[59] The fact that the method for the theological teaching is a parable, an extended metaphor, does not mitigate the oppressive nature of the social phenomena and ideals of which the metaphor makes use. "A memorable metaphor has the power to bring two separate domains into cognitive and emotional relation by using language directly appropriate to the one as a lens for seeing the other."[60] The cruel existence of the tortured slave that the metaphors rely upon is precisely useful to help the audience visualize what the kingdom expects of its subjects. It is no accident that slavery is the chosen lens for conceptualizing the "kingdom of the heavens."

ed. Fernando F. Segovia and R. S. Sugirtharajah (New York/London: T&T Clark, 2009), 69–103, at 99–100.

56. Fernando F. Segovia, "Introduction: Configurations, Approaches, Findings, Stances," in Segovia and Sugirtharajah, eds., *Postcolonial Commentary*, 1–68, at 32, 52. See also Fernando F. Segovia, "Postcolonial Criticism and the Gospel of Matthew," in *Methods for Matthew*, ed. Mark Allan Powell (Cambridge, UK: Cambridge University Press, 2009), 194–238, esp. 221–28.

57. Musa Dube, *Postcolonial Feminist Interpretation of the Bible* (St. Louis: Chalice, 2000), 133.

58. M. Eugene Boring, "Matthew," in *The New Interpreter's Bible*, vol. 8: *General Articles on the New Testament, Matthew, Mark*, ed. Leander Keck (Nashville: Abingdon, 1995), 104.

59. Perhaps Cyrus the Great of Persia was the first and only King to refuse to build his empire on the backs of eslaved persons, employing skilled craftspersons and laborers whom he paid a fair wage. Cyrus conquered Babylon and freed the Jewish people from slavery. Cambyses, Darius the Great, Xerxes and Artaxerxes may have followed in Cyrus's footsteps refusing to enslave those peoples they conquered.

60. Max Black, *Metaphors: Studies in Language and Philosophy* (Ithaca: Cornell University Press, 1962), 236.

Conclusion

I have argued that the parable of the ten virgins is a slave parable and is part of a trilogy. In all three parables the master–slave system with the trustworthy tortured slave and the harsh master is touted as an ideal to be imitated by those wishing to participate in the kingdom of the heavens. I have also argued that the expected preparedness predicated on being in a constant state of wakefulness or sleep deprivation is a form of torture integral to slave life, and to contemporary black life in America. Through the tortured slave body the truth of his subordination and the master's superiority was daily extracted. On such tortured bodies kingdoms, colonies, churches, and universities have been built.[61] I propose that the iconic kingdom rhetoric should be rejected. Should our theology be ground in such cruelty and barbarism? DuBois writes that a "principal motive of [political] torture … is control, the domination of an unpalatable truth. That truth may be communism, nationalism, democracy, any number of threatening political beliefs that disrupt the unity, the unblemished purity and wholeness of the state, or of any entity analogous to the unitary philosophical subject."[62] That "unpalatable truth" may also be egalitarianism or justice, which threatens the privilege of those who benefit from the injustice of racism, sexism, classism, heterosexism, and other -isms in society at large, in our churches or in our educational and theological institutions.

---

61. See Craig Steven Wilder, *Ebony and Ivy: Race, Slavery, and the Troubled History of America's Universities* (New York: Bloomsbury, 2014).
62. DuBois, *Torture and Truth*, 149.

Dis-membering, Sexual Violence, and Confinement: A Womanist Intersectional Reading of the Story of the Levite's Wife (Judges 19)

The[1] story of the gang rape and mutilation of a Levite's secondary wife in Judges 19 is indeed a "text of terror," as Phyllis Trible has argued.[2] Texts of terror reflect, describe and critique the violence humans inflict upon one another, as well as our ignorance, complicity, and culpability in the brutality and victimization of women and others. Sometimes it is the Divine who is depicted as terrorizing women and their children or as sanctioning violence among humans. We often rationalize that the violence we commit is necessary and different from the violence committed by the internal and external other and between the other. For example Representative Sean Duff (R-Wis) recently argued that the terrorist threats from the "Middle East are an existen-

---

1. By permission of Ashland Theological Seminary, this essay is a revision of "Reading the Story of the Levite's Concubine through the Lens of Modern-Day Sex Trafficking," *Ashland Theological Journal* 41 (a non-peer-review journal) (2009): 15–34.
2. Phyllis Trible, *Texts of Terror: Literary-Feminist Readings of Biblical Narratives*, Overtures to Biblical Theology (Minneapolis: Fortress Press, 1984).

tial threat to the United States and totally different for white domestic terrorists," the latter of which the government "can't do anything about."[3] In a patriarchal society dominated by white males, "attacks by white people . . . aren't as big a problem," but statistics demonstrate otherwise.[4] When asked, about the nine African American women and men murdered (six women, three men; three others injured) in the Emmanuel African Methodist Episcopal Church in Charleston, SC, on June 17, 2015, by self-proclaimed white supremacists Dylann Roof, Congressman Duff downplayed that act of domestic terrorism, pointing out the taking down of the confederate flag as a positive outcome. Violence against women and minorities and especially poor women of color is often minimized or dismissed.

This chapter offers a womanist reading of the story of the unnamed Levite's secondary wife (or slave),[5] focusing on the phenomenon and epidemic of sexual violence and the incarceration of poor black women. In dialogue with Beth E. Richie's book *Arrested Justice*, about black women, violence, and incarceration,[6] I read the physical mutilation and murder of the Levite's secondary wife as the ultimate tragic culmination of a lifetime of abuse, including physical confinement.[7] When people live in societies that subordinate and oppress them because of their gender, sexuality, race/ethnicity and/or class, without the benefit of appropriate and equitable protections and just interventions, they live constantly with the threat and are subjected to polymorphic violence, mutilation and premature death. Daily subjection to violence can assuredly prevent one from escaping poverty.[8] Most incarcerated women are poor and women of color who have a history of being physically and/or sexually abused prior to their incarceration, which often continues while they are imprisoned and placed

3. Amanda Terkel, "GOP Congressman Insists White Terrorists Attacks are Totally Different," The Huffington Post, February 7, 2017. http://www.huffingtonpost.com/entry/sean-duffy-terrorism_us_589a081ce4b0c1284f28854c.
4. Terkel, "GOP Congressman Insists." See Sarah Frostenson, "Most Terrorists Attacks in the US are Committed by Americans—Not Foreigners," Vox, September 9, 2016. http://www.vox.com/2015/11/23/9765718/domestic-terrorism-threat.
5. It is similar to the story of Lot's daughters in Genesis 19:1–11.
6. Beth E. Richie, *Arrested Justice: Black Women, Violence, and America's Prison Nation* (New York: New York University Press, 2012).
7. For other readings of this story that focus on dismemberment, see Joy A. Schroeder, "Dismembering The Adulteress: Sixteenth-Century Commentary on the Narrative of the Levite's Concubine (Judges 19–21)," *Seminary Ridge Review* 9, no. 2 (2007): 5–24; Julie Faith Parker, "Re-membering the Dismembered: Piecing Together Meaning from Stories of Women and Body Parts in Ancient Near Eastern Literature," *Biblical Interpretation* 23, no. 2 (2015): 174–90.
8. See Gary A. Haugen, *The Locus Effect. Why the End of Poverty Requires the End of Violence* (New York and London: Oxford University Press, 2015).

under male guards. Re-victimization also occurs when abused and/ or stigmatized women seek justice and/or refuge. This re-victimization is part of the process of *dis*-membering. The *dis*-membering of the Levite's secondary wife, and the contemporary *dis*-membering of African American women and other women and people of color, especially the poor, should be understood not as a single event but as a dynamic dehumanizing and disenfranchising process; it is an accumulative trajectory of assaults whereby basic rights and protections are violated or denied, inflicting and allowing for physical abuse, confinement, mutilation, and early death. In America's prison nation, certain women are rendered more vulnerable than others. Richie states

> Black women who do not fit into the traditional image of an innocent victim because they are an adolescent defendant charged with neonaticide, a lesbian who resists a sexually aggressive stranger, or a resident of public housing who is a victim of police brutality rather than interpersonal violence, will not receive the protection of a prison nation. And, if she is a prostitute, an active substance abuser, a woman who is has lost custody of her children because of neglect, an undocumented immigrant, or simply a woman who has learned that the state will not protect her, she is even *less likely* to be served by the criminal legal system's very general response to male violence. Indeed, they are not "real women."[9]

Reading *Ênmishpat* Intersectionally

In an earlier essay, I read this story through the lens of human trafficking, giving little attention to race. In this revision, I focus on the intersectionality of race/ethnicity, gender, and class; the interpretive lens, analytical categories, and questions we raise matter. Neither the Levite nor his wife are named. Perhaps, her anonymity is a literary strategy, as J. Cheryl Exum argues "for distancing the reader from the character."[10] That depends upon the reader. Pamela Reis states that anonymity of both the Levite and his lesser wife "reflects the increasing dehumanization and disintegration of society." Prior to chapter 19 a few characters are still being given names, but in chapter 19 "decency and order have deteriorated to a nadir in which no one deserves the humanizing elevation of a name."[11] But such societal deterioration has

---

9. Richie, *Arrested Justice*, 124.
10. J. Cheryl Exum, *Fragmented Women: Feminist (Sub)versions of Biblical Narratives*, Journal for the Study of the Old Testament Supplement Series 163 (Sheffield, UK: Sheffield University Press, 1993), 176.
11. Pamela Reis, "The Levite's Concubine: New Light on a Dark Story," *Scandinavian Journal of the Old Testament* 20, no. 1 (2006): 125–46, at 127 and 130.

a more adverse impact on the most vulnerable in any society—poor othered-women and their children. Following what Wil Gafney has done for Zipporah's mother and her six sisters, which is to honor their presence by naming them, I will, for the purpose of this essay, name the Levite's secondary wife 'Ênmishpat, meaning in Hebrew "there was/is no justice."[12] The story demonstrates that there was no justice for the Levite's secondary wife.

Reading the story of the *dis*-membering of 'Ênmishpat through a womanist intersectional lens highlights the complexity of social divisions that are interrelated and that mutually affect an individual or group of peoples. The social divisions of race/ethnicity, gender, sexuality, and class and the oppressions associated such classifications or identities have dire consequences for poor African American women and other peoples of color. A significant impact of the lingering legacy of slavery, of Jim/Jane Crow, of systemic discrimination, disenfranchisement on poor women of color is a sociopolitical *dis*-membering. Just like enslaved persons experience a social death, as Orlando Patterson argues, the impact of systemic multidimensional and interlocking oppressions that deprive people of access to certain resources, rights and protections that are primarily afforded to members of the dominant culture and classes is a kind of social death or *dis*-membering. Poor people of color are denied ordinary human rights and dignities like access to clean affordable water, a living equitable wage, protection from abusive spouses or intimate partners, justice in both private and public or domestic and civil spaces. A disregard for and a disrespect or in slang "*diss*-ing" (manifested by a silencing and rendering them invisible and a refusal to treat them with ordinary human dignity) is the precursor to and the foundation for denying black women and other women of color, full human and civil rights and membership privileges in both the private and public spheres. As Beth Richie writes, "because of their over-representation in disadvantaged social positions, Black women are more likely to have low-paying jobs, live in unsafe public housing, be forced to travel on inefficient public transportation, and otherwise be left in harm's way because of their class status; they are more vulnerable to all forms of abuse, and it is more likely that community-level aggression toward them will be minimized or ignored."[13] This social subordination, repression, and/or oppression

---

12. Wil Gafney, "A Womanist Midrash on Zipporah," in *I Found God in Me*, ed. Mitzi J. Smith (Eugene, OR: Cascade, 2015), 131–57. Gafney names Zipporah's mother Poriyah, meaning "fruitful," and names the sisters Lya, Aminah, Minnah, Taima, Yarah, and Zizah.

functions as a *dis*-membering that too often results in a physical and social mutilation and premature death at the hands of others with impunity. Death is the final outcome of *dis*-membering. To *dis*-member someone is to systemically deny them social equality and to confine them to unprotected and abusive spaces and relationships; it is to remove them from participation in social relationships that they would otherwise enjoy if they were free and respected as human beings. It is to take away their power of choice over their own bodies and their access to the best necessary resources for themselves and their children.

'Ênmishpat's story relates a raw display of violence and brutality inflicted upon a young woman whose gender, social status or class, and ethnicity afford her no protectors. She is eventually and ultimately the victim of men governed solely by their own insatiable lusts. The sociohistorical context is broadly described, in brief, by six, previously spoken, words: "there was no king in Israel" (19:1; 17:6; 18:1).[14] 'Ênmishpat's story (and the book of Judges) concludes with the addendum, "In those days there was no king in Israel; all the people did what was right in their own eyes" (21:25).[15] The story might be understood in terms of nation-lust, demonstrating the extent to which men will go in pursuit of nationalism for the protection of men and their property. With or without a king, too many men in patriarchal societies, where equity and justice are contingent upon one's gender, class, sexuality, ethnicity/race, do as they please and what pleases them. Prior to the double Levirate priest narratives (chs. 17–18 and 19–21), the aphorism reads: "the Israelites did what was evil in the sight of the Lord" (2:11; 3:7, 12; 4:1; 10:6; 13:1; cp. 17:6; 21:25).[16] And the Levites were no exception. The prevalence of such moral individualism in a patriarchal, misogynistic, class-conscious, and/or xenophobic society results in the *dis*-membering of the most vulnerable members of society.

---

13. Richie, *Arrested Justice*, 43.
14. 1 and 2 Samuel, which narrate the selection of Israel's first and second kings, Saul and David, follows the book of Judges in the Masoretic Text (MT); but in the Greek text (LXX), the book of Ruth intervenes. Perhaps the stories in Judges amount to religio-political propaganda in support of a monarchy.
15. All Bible quotations are from the New Revised Standard Version unless otherwise noted.
16. The cycle of apostasy, judgment, cry for help, and God's deliverance by a judge is present up until Judges 17, when the pattern changes and we have the double Levite priest stories.

Dis-membering: Secondary-Wife Status and
Accompanying Abuses

'Ênmishpat is the Levite's secondary or lesser wife (*pîlegesh*). She is a *taken* secondary wife; she is the gendered object of the Levite's right and decision to take her (19:2). Trible writes, "He is subject; she, object. He controls her. How he acquired her we do not know; that he owns her is certain."[17] Nevertheless, it is not unusual in the Hebrew Bible for a woman, especially secondary wife, to be taken (e.g., Gen 16:3; 20:2–3).[18] She will be taken to the tent (*'ōhēl*) or place (*maqôm*) of her Ephraimite husband as his lesser wife (cf. Judg 8:31). The first act of violence or *dis*-membering is the social categorization of 'Ênmishpat as a secondary or lesser wife, relegating her to a lower social status and laying the foundation for and justifying further acts of violence. She lives with a degree of instability and uncertainty; she can be replaced by a primary wife and doubly subordinated to another woman as well as to her husband. She is a placeholder, perhaps until the Levite finds the wife he wanted or preferred from among his own tribe.

If the anonymity of both the Levite and 'Ênmishpat is strategic, the nomenclature identifying the provenance of the pair is intentional as well: He is identified as a Levite living in the hill country of Ephraim and she is from Bethlehem. While the designation of the husband as "Levite" carries some social and ethnic capital given its connection with the priesthood, Bethlehem does not yet possess the same social capital. He is of a higher social class (priest) by nature of his tribal affiliation (Levite) and gender. In our story, the dissonance between the lesser wife's and the Levite's social status is clear. Although both the Levite and 'Ênmishpat's are anonymous, their social class is foregrounded. God consecrated the Levites to serve as priests (Num 1:48–54). The foregrounding of the Levite's social position within Israel is similarly achieved in the preceding story of the unnamed Levite (Judges 17–18). They are associated with leadership in established religious circles. The fact that this unnamed man is identified as a Levite might prejudice some readers in favor of the Levite so that they are willing to overlook or mitigate any questionable behavior attributed to him. Or the Levite's status may motivate some readers to view 'Ênmish-

---

17. Trible, *Texts of Terror*, 66.
18. In the Hagar story, it is Sarah, her mistress, who takes and gives her concubine to Abram (Gen 16:3).

pat as the guilty party in the marriage because she is of lower-class status.

When a link is created between social status and ideas of familiarity, persons who attain to levels of social status based on positions of authority held in a society are considered as safer, less dangerous and morally superior to persons of lower social status. But the elite and persons of authority in any society or community are as capable of immorality and violence against women and girls as are any other members of a society.

Gafney argues that the lesser wife's status as secondary wife means "she and any children would not be entitled to support from her husband, making her financially vulnerable. It is possible the Levite entered into a secondary union with her because she was not a Levite woman, reserving the prerogative of primary marriage for a tribeswoman."[19] Like 'Ênmishpat, African American women experience racial/ethnic subordination and economic disparity that sets in motion their *dis*-membering. According to the Center for American Progress, "African American women continue to have higher rates of unemployment than white women and continue to have lower amounts of weekly usual earnings and median wealth compared to their male counterparts and white women. These disparities leave a growing portion of our population more vulnerable to poverty and its implications."[20] Poor women and children are disproportionately subjected to violence.

Dis-membering: Circumscription of Agency and Absence of Sanctuary

'Ênmishpat leaves her husband's residence and returns to her father's house.[21] The reason why 'Ênmishpat leaves her husband is linguistically ambiguous. 'Ênmishpat either played the harlot (*znch*) (according to the Masoretic Text [MT]) or she became angry (*ōrgisthē* in the Greek text or LXX; *znh* in the Hebrew) with her husband (19:2).[22] According to

---

19. Wil Gafney, "What Judges 19 Has to Say about Domestic Violence," *Sojourners* (October 5, 2015), https://sojo.net/print/217296.

20. Maria Guerra, "Fact Sheet: The State of African American Women in the United States," Center for American Progress, November 7, 2013, https://www.americanprogress.org/issues/race/report/2013/11/07/79165/fact-sheet-the-state-of-african-american-women-in-the-united-states.

21. Mieke Bal, in *Death and Dissymmetry: The Politics of Coherence in the Book of Judges* (Chicago: University of Chicago Press, 1988), 80–93, argues that the concubine lived in the father's home and not with her husband and the Levite's taking of her from her father's home represents an attempt to transform the nature of their relationship.

Trible, "The story itself allows either reading."[23] Reis has argued that the woman was unfaithful *for* him; "[t]he Levite was prostituting his wife."[24] If the Levite was prostituting his wife, as Reis argues, and the concubine expected to be treated with respect, under such an arrangement the concubine would have reason to become angry and leave. Or perhaps the concubine has been falsely accused of fornication by her husband who has himself been unfaithful; projecting one's guilt upon an innocent partner is not an uncommon form of intimate partner abuse. Emotional and/or physical abuse could be the cause of 'Ênmishpat's anger and departure (see Deut 22:15–21). As Trible has observed, "the narrative censures no one for the concubine's departure," but the story hints at the Levite's guilt. The Levite's guilt might explain why he waited four months to go and "speak tenderly to her heart."[25] Gafney argues that "the ambiguity is likely intentional, making it possible for some readers to blame her for leaving her husband, and therefore whatever befalls her ... it's the original form of slut-shaming ... [and] the first act of violence against her."[26] It is an aspect of 'Ênmishpat's *dis*-membering. In any case, 'Ênmishpat is angry enough to leave her husband's home and assume the risk of finding (or not finding) temporary or permanent sanctuary in her father's house. Perhaps 'Ênmishpat's flight came after a longer period of abuse. *Dis*-membering denies 'Ênmishpat's full humanity and access to basic human rights and protections. *Dis*-membering also seeks to normalize violence. 'Ênmishpat's flight is a rejection of this normalizing tendancy.

Consequently 'Ênmishpat is now both a lesser wife and a fugitive. Unlike Hagar, 'Ênmishpat does not voluntarily return to her master; she is retrieved.[27] The Levite will never relinquish his right to *take* his secondary wife, to take 'Ênmishpat for a second time. In fact, the many references to the Levite as "son-in-law" or husband (*'îš*) and to the father as "father-in-law" foreground the legal relationship that continues to exist among the parties and that transcends geographical and domestic space (19:4, 5, 6, 9). Having left without her husband's permission and without being put out of his house (although it is possible she

---

22. The MT says she committed fornication (*znh*), but the rest of the text implies guilt on the part of the Levite and not the woman, in my opinion. The LXX, on which I rely, says she became angry (*ōrgisthē*) (Hebrew: *znch*).
23. Trible, *Texts of Terror*, 67.
24. Reis, "The Levite's Concubine," 129.
25. Trible, *Texts of Terror*, 67.
26. Gafney, "What Judges 19 Has to Say about Domestic Violence."
27. See Delores S. Williams, *Sisters in the Wilderness: The Challenge of Womanist God-Talk* (Maryknoll, NY: Orbis, 1993).

was), 'Ênmishpat is a fugitive, no matter how long her Levite husband waits before retrieving her.

It is only when 'Ênmishpat flees to her father's house that she is referred to as a young woman (*na'ar*) and only for the purpose of identifying the father (19:3, 4, 5, 6, 8, 9). Perhaps the language shows that she is still his little girl, and that he will do what he can for her without dishonoring himself or jeopardizing male fraternity and hegemonic patriarchal authority over women. Or perhaps it shows that she like other young women taken as wives have no sanctuary from abusive husbands. In the grammar of the text, the young woman is present either as a possessive pronoun ("her") or as the second noun in a Hebrew construct pair ("the father of the young woman"). Her grammatical position, behind her father, serves to identify a father in relation to his daughter, rendering him present and her subordinate.[28] In the story, she is invisible and yet in plain (over)sight of men; she is silent and silenced as a result of her subordinate social status. The silencing of women is a form of abuse. 'Ênmishpat's silencing is part of her *dis*-membering.[29] Women and children (and some men) who fear speaking up or who are not permitted to tell their own stories and to speak about their own oppressions and victimization without censure and further victimization suffer in silence and sometimes indefinitely.

The Levite will retrieve and transport or traffic 'Ênmishpat without her consent, because he can. Four months after 'Ênmishpat's escape, her husband the Levite exercises his privilege and right to pursue her; he travels to Bethlehem of Judah to retrieve her from her father's house. 'Ênmishpat has no permanent sanctuary; all the men in her life are either complicit gatekeepers of patriarchal violence or perpetrators. Human trafficking (a term often used to describe modern-day slavery) flourishes as its victims remain "invisible" to others.[30] Children stay enslaved for extended periods of time since no one identifies them as enslaved. Their enslavement is invisible to their communities, but this is the paradox. According to David Batstone, "slaves toil in the public eye."[31] 'Ênmishpat's victimization remains invisible; her victimization is concealed behind ideas of patriarchal normalcy, of what can occur between a man and his wife without intervention. Thus, domes-

---

28. Likewise, the father only exists in relation to his daughter or his son-in-law.
29. Reis, in "The Levite's Concubine," 136, argues that the woman's insufferable predicament is "pitied and respected by the text."
30. David Batstone, *Not for Sale: The Return of the Global Slave Trade—and How We Can Fight It* (New York: HarperCollins, 2007), 268.
31. Ibid., 7.

tic relationships and spaces can be used as a pretext or context for normalized abuse; in fact, labeling any violence as "domestic" mitigates its impact and gives it normalcy.

'Ēnmishpat exercised agency when she left her husband/master's home and traveled to her father's house. Her abandonment of her husband can be perceived as an act of survival.[32] The cost of staying outweighed the potential consequences of flight. Her father does not send her back; maybe he knows something we don't know. Or maybe the fact that he does not send his daughter back confirms that he does not consider her actions unreasonable or unjustified. We might see her flight, her attempt to find refuge from her husband, as her way of reporting her crime in the only way available to her. "Several [contemporary] studies have shown that marital rape is often more violent and frequent than other rape and is less commonly reported."[33]

It is clear that even if 'Ēnmishpat's flight was justified, her husband could (and did) forcefully reclaim her[34] from her father's house. Her agency is circumscribed. 'Ēnmishpat's victimization did not compel her father to transgress social rules regarding men and their wives/property. The same agency the concubine exercised to leave her husband would not allow her to stay indefinitely in her father's home. In modern-day trafficking, as in all abusive relationships, the message communicated to the victim is that any attempt to reassume control will be punished.[35]

The relationship between agency and victimization is a hotly debated issue among advocates of human sex-trafficking victims. The question is whether victimization and agency should be seen as contradictory terms. Some believe that if one can exercise agency, then one cannot be a victim. Liz Kelly notes that when women exercise agency

32. The concubine wife's story is not unlike the story of Samson and his first wife (Judg 14:1–15:6). In fact, it may be a mirror image of our story. In his anger Samson abandons his first wife because she betrayed his trust, and he returns to *his* father's home. After some time, Samson attempts to reclaim his wife, but because his father-in-law was certain that Samson had rejected his daughter, he gave her to another man. Both father-in-law and (ex-)wife are murdered by foreigners, the Philistines, due to Samuel's actions. Of course, in our story it is the concubine wife who is angry, returns to her father's home, and is reclaimed; like Samson's wife, the Levite's concubine is murdered, but by perverted "brothers" and not by foreigners.

33. Richie, *Arrested Justice*, 31.

34. For a discussion about the issue of consent and trafficking in the context of negotiations leading to the eighty-country signing of The Trafficking Protocol in Palermo, Italy, in December 2000, see Jo Doezema, "Who Gets to Choose? Coercion, Consent and the UN Trafficking Protocol," *Gender and Development* 10 (2002): 20–27. See also Kamala Kempadoo and Jo Doezema, eds., *Global Sex Workers: Rights, Resistance and Redefinition* (New York/London: Routledge, 1998).

35. Kevin Bales and Ron Soodalter, *The Slave Next Door: Human Trafficking and Slavery in America Today* (Berkeley: University of California Press, 2010), 78.

in the context of domestic violence we do not deny their victimization, even though they may return to their abusers, but different logic is applied to trafficked women. If trafficked women exercise any agency, they are not considered victims.[36] But Kelly argues that "[a]gency is exercised in context, and contexts are always more or less constrained by material and other factors."[37] In a patriarchal society where women's bodies are subject to male authority and male authority is ultimate authority, women (and other subordinates) have no places of refuge; thus, agency is circumscribed and complex.

Dis-membering: When *Family* and the Familiar Are Most Dangerous

'Ênmishpat's story is replete with images and language of familiarity. Richie states that most assaults against black women are more likely to occur in close proximity to home, in their neighborhoods, around familiar surroundings than in a different neighborhood; women who live in low-income communities rarely venture far from their own neighborhoods.[38] Family and familiarity can and often does render risk and danger invisible or at least unimaginable. What is *family* or familiar and therefore often normal requires little caution or critique. Ideas of personal or communal safety and minimization of risk are often based on familiarity. Normally expected behavior, particularly normalcy practiced by authoritative or dominant persons or institutions, can camouflage or render invisible oppression and violence. In contexts of perceived familiarity and/or normalcy, oppression and brutality against women and children can more easily occur with little or no interference. We warn our children, and rightly so, to beware of strangers. But traffickers in human flesh are often not strangers. Every year thousands of women and children, drawn from every corner of the world, are recruited, drafted and detained into modern-day sex slavery in the United States.[39]

Among the ancients, the most vulnerable in society (conquered and

---

36. Liz Kelly, "The Wrong Debate: Reflections on Why Force Is Not the Key Issue with Respect to Trafficking in Women for Sexual Exploitation," *Feminist Review* 73 (2003): 139–44, at 142.
37. Ibid., 143.
38. Richie, *Arrested Justice*, 39.
39. While I am aware that human trafficking includes debt, agricultural, and domestic trafficking, etc., my emphasis in this article is on sex trafficking, although other forms of modern slavery often overlap. A person could be held against their will under threat of violence initially for the purpose of working in a sweatshop or goldmine or as a domestic worker or tomato picker and later be subjected to sexual abuse.

subjugated men, women, and children) could be enslaved. In modern-day sex slavery the most vulnerable in society are preyed upon. As in ancient slavery, modern-day slave owners enjoy free access to enslaved bodies for labor, profit, and sexual satisfaction. Since slavery is now illegal in the United States,[40] but not unconstitutional, enslavers utilize cunning and deceptive means to acquire bodies to be enslaved as objects of male sexual desire and abuse. Enslavers employ the pretense and the situation of familiarity to lure women and children into sex slavery.

Familiarity has to do with proximity.[41] By proximity I mean nearness in terms of familial relationship, ethnicity, culture, geography, social status, religious affiliation, and/or gender. People who we consider proximate to us are those most like us. Ideas of in-group homogeneity are linked to perceptions of familiarity.[42]

'Ênmishpat's story linguistically demonstrates familial and familiar relationships between her and the men in her life and between and among the men: "her father," "her husband," "father of the young woman," "father-in-law," "son-in-law," "wife," "brothers," and "children [sons] of Israel." Reis has aptly noted that "the six repetitions of the phrase 'father of the woman' hammer the woman's vulnerability and the father's family relationship into one's consciousness and prompt the reader to contrast the man's bond with his behavior. He is her father, father, father, . . . but he does not act like a father."[43] Or perhaps he does act like a father, a father conflicted by his love for his daughter and his privileged membership within a patriarchal society. While many horror stories of human trafficking can be told, most sex trafficking is "mundane, involving every day, routine power and control relationships," similar to domestic violence and child sexual abuse.[44]

---

40. Congressional laws enacted in the last decade of the eighteenth century and the first decade of the nineteenth century have prohibited *de jure* the transport of slaves into America and the supply of ships to the slave trade. Those laws also permitted the confiscation of slave ships and for the U.S. Navy to seize slave ships as well. While slavery *de jure* ended with the enactment of the Thirteenth Amendment, slavery *de facto* continued and in some ways has never disappeared from America. Bales, *The Slave Next Door*, 150–51.

41. J. Z. Smith employs this term but notes that proximity is a basis for othering; the proximate other, the one most like us, is the one most threatening to us. See his essay "What a Difference a Difference Makes," in *"To See Ourselves as Others See Us": Christians, Jews, "Others" in Late Antiquity*, ed. Jacob Neusner and Ernest S. Frerichs (Chico, CA: Scholars, 1985), 3–48.

42. Penelope J. Oakes, S. Alexander Haslam, Brenda Morrison, and Diana Grace, "Becoming an In-Group: Reexamining the Impact of Familiarity on Perceptions of Group Homogeneity," *Social Psychology Quarterly* 58, no. 1 (1995): 52–61.

43. Reis, "The Levite's Concubine," 133.

44. Kelly, "The Wrong Debate," 140.

Dis-membering: Male Fraternity and the Eclipsing of a Woman's Voice and Choice

'Ênmishpat is the only woman in her father's house when the Levite arrives with his servant boy to retrieve her. Fraternity among men allows for male enjoyment and self-gratification to the exclusion of a woman's well-being. In a patriarchal society a woman's well-being is subordinated to and defined in relation to the needs and enjoyment of men; her voice and choice are eclipsed. Enjoyment (social and sexual) is the privilege of males in this story. We would not know the Levite's secondary wife was in her father's home if the narrator had not told us so. She is never included in the eating-drinking-and-spending-the-night scenes. "Neither food nor drink nor companionship attends the female, but the males enjoy it all."[45] Fraternity among men finds expression in the language of eating, drinking, and spending the night—the son-in-law under the father-in-law's roof.[46] Reis notes that a literal translation of the Hebrew would render 19:6 as "And they sat and they ate, two of them together, *and they drank*" (Reis's emphasis), "so that the reader suspects drinking to excess."[47] This collocation of phrases does not necessarily indicate inebriation among men. The emphasis could be upon the camaraderie and conversation that takes place when two men share food to the intentional exclusion of all others in the household. This phrase, "the two of them together," it should be noted, also appears in the MT when no drinking is mentioned (19:8). Also, later in the story when the Levite and the old man eat together, it is explicitly stated that they are sharing wine, but the phrase "the two of them together" is absent from the MT (19:19–21).

While the young man (*na'ar*) traveling with the Levite is absent from the story until the Levite leaves to retrieve his wife and is rendered silent in the father-in-law's house, the young man does eventually speak. Thus, every male in the story, speaks for himself. When the travelers arrive at Jebus (later Jerusalem), the young man attempts to convince the Levite to stay the night in Jebus so as not to risk a late-night arrival in Gibeah.[48] Perhaps the young man knows by expe-

---

45. Trible, *Texts of Terror*, 68.
46. Although the term *father-in law* is used to describe the relation between the Levite and the young woman's father, a concubine did not have the same legal or social status as a wife; she is a secondary wife.
47. Reis, "The Levite's Concubine," 134.
48. Both Jebus and Gibeah were allotted as inheritances to the tribe of Benjamin (Josh 18:21–28), but the Benjaminites failed to drive out the Jebusites (Judg 1:21).

rience what awaits men, and men with subordinate women, in Gibeah. In fact, when they arrive in Jebus, the narrator notes that the Levite has a pair of saddled donkeys and his secondary wife; the young man is not mentioned as among the Levite's property as previously noted (19:10; cf. 19:3). Unequivocally, the young man is servant and the Levite is his master (*'adōni*). Vocal intellectual agency is connected with maleness in the story. Of course, the Levite exercises his class privilege and rejects his young male servant's admonition, insisting on crossing over (*'ābar*) into Gibeah or Ramah because the Jebusites are not children of Israel (19:12–14). It will be from an Ephraimite sojourner's home that 'Ênmishpat's husband will discard her to be ravished by some Israelite "brothers" (19:23–25).

The Levite leaves his father-in-law's house with 'Ênmishpat in tow, returning to Ephraim. The narrative gives the impression that the Levite's actions are routine and void of tenderness—in spite of the father's attempts to appeal to his son-in-law's heart. Just as he got up (*qǔm*) to retrieve his concubine after she had been gone for four months, he got up (*qǔm*) and left his father-in-law's home. And after the brutal sexual assault on his concubine, the Levite will get up (*qǔm*) and leave there, too. Once a woman's choice and voice are taken away, men can do whatever they want to her body!

Dis-membering: The Pretext of "Speaking to the Heart"

In the midst of male fraternity we find the language of the heart. The Levite traveled to his father-in-law's house to speak to the heart of 'Ênmishpat (19:3). Similarly, Shechem spoke to Dinah's heart after he raped her (Gen 34:3; cf. Hos 2:14–15). The husband does all the talking; he speaks to her, not with her. He does not ask her what she wants? Abusive men seldom, if ever, are interested in what their partners think, feel or want. Erik Eynikel has noted that if the Levite's wife had committed adultery, her sin would have been punishable by death rather than by "speaking to her heart."[49] In contemporary society we know that men who abuse women (or any abuser regardless of gender or sexuality) often feign remorse and "speak tenderly" to those they continue to abuse, especially if the threat or possibility exists that the victim will publicize the abuse, elicit sympathy (and perhaps intervention) from outsiders, and press charges. Men (and women) as abusers

---

49. Erik Eynikel Nijmegen, "Judges 19–21, An 'Appendix': Rape, Murder, War and Abduction," *Communio Viatorum* 47, no. 2 (2005): 101–15, at 104.

of their significant others have been known to express sorrow for their actions while simultaneously blaming their victims for provoking them to become violent. Men who speak tenderly to their wives will also sacrifice their wives to protect their reputations and positions within society. Often intimate partner abuse is the last resort for men who believe that an insubordinate wife is threatening their putative, sacralized position as head or master of the household.

While the Levite attempts to speak to his concubine's heart, the father endeavors to influence the Levite's heart. After the Levite has spent three days in his father-in-law's home, the father prevails upon his son-in-law to stay another *day*, "to refresh your heart with a piece of bread" (19:5; my translation). On the fourth day, the two men share a meal and some drink. And once their appetites are satisfied, the father encourages the son-in-law to stay another *night* because "it will be good for your heart" (19:6). This day/night pattern is repeated in verses 8 and 9. Perhaps this night language ("it will be good for your heart") is an indirect reference to the danger that lurks in the night, which the Levite (and by extension the young woman) might avoid if he spends the night. Maybe it is a veiled appeal to the son-in-law to be good to his wife. But abusers are seldom rational or interested in the safety of their victims. The father's hospitable treatment of the son-in-law may be perceived as an attempt to ensure her safety and to convince the Levite that his secret is safe.[50]

Dis-membering: Confined and on the Road of No Return

Once she is taken away from her father's home, 'Ênmishpat experiences a kind of confinement. She is taken against her will and her crime is fleeing abuse, abdicating her position as unconditionally submissive secondary wife. 'Ênmishpat is taken into custody by the one with whom she became angry enough to risk the consequences of flight and homelessness, not knowing whether or how long her father's house would be the sanctuary she sought.[51] Once he takes her from the place in which she sought refuge, from her temporary safe house, she is his prisoner to do with her as he wishes; she will be confined to remain within her husband's grasp and sight and subjected to further sexual

---

50. Koala Jones-Warsaw, "Toward a Womanist Hermeneutic: A Reading of Judges 19–21," in *A Feminist Companion to Judges*, ed. Athalya Brenner (Sheffield, UK: Sheffield University Press, 1993), 175.

51. Bal (*Death and Dissymmetry*) argues that the concubine lived in the father's home and not with her husband, and the Levite's taking of her from her father's home represents an attempt to transform the nature of their relationship.

abuse. In 2014, more than "200,000 women were imprisoned in the US . . . at least 15 percent of incarcerated females have been the victims of prison sexual assault" by male prison staff. Although they make up only 7 percent of state prison populations, they are 46 percent of sexual-abuse victims.[52]

The Levite will transport 'Ênmishpat to a land and people that are familiar to him, and there she will be trafficked. Human trafficking affects all races, nationalities, and genders. Nevertheless, over half of the cases of sex trafficking in the United States involve black children. People of color were reportedly seventy-seven percent of victims in alleged human trafficking incidents in the U.S.[53]

Dis-membering: Hospitality is Limited to Men at the Expense of Women's Bodies

The Levite's penultimate destination will be the home of a fellow Ephraimite. The sun has gone down when they are near Gibeah, Benjaminite territory. They sit in the city square in the dark, but not one of the natives offers to receive the travelers. Hospitality (at least for the Levite) will be offered by one whose background is familiar and/or similar to the Levite's; his host will be an old Ephraimite man sojourning in Gibeah—a "homeboy." "The tribal town becomes the alien place . . . one from the territory of the master, will provide the hospitality that the natives do not offer."[54]

Again the familiar or proximate are considered safe and worthy of hospitality. Geographical language indicating the familiar and unfamiliar (foreign) continues to be significant in our story. Both the Levite and the old man are sojourners; the old man is a sojourner in Gibeah who originated from the hill country of Ephraim and the Levite is a sojourner from Ephraim traveling through Gibeah (19:1, 16). Jebus, where the Levite refused to spend the night, was considered a dangerous foreign city where the people are not Israelites (19:12). But Gibeah where the Benjaminites dwell is a place where fellow Israelites live and thus a place of familiarity and fraternity; it is a safe place for spending the night. The hospitality of "brothers" is preferred to turning aside

52. Christina Piecora, "Female Inmates and Sexual Assault," *Jurist*, Student Commentary (September 14, 2014), http://www.jurist.org/dateline/2014/09/christina-piecora-female-inmates.php.

53. Jamaal Bell, "Race and Human Trafficking in U.S.: Unclear but Undeniable," The Huffington Post, May 25, 2011. http://www.huffingtonpost.com/jamaal-bell/race-and-human-traffickin_b_5697 95.html.

54. Trible, *Texts of Terror*, 71.

among foreigners. Ironically, the old man warns the Levite not to sleep in the public square of the Israelite town (19:20). While the old man could travel from the field and back home every evening unmolested, a traveler cannot remain safely in the public square in the night (19:16).

Intragroup notions of superiority and security foster a domestic versus inter-national dichotomy regarding among whom and where danger exists. The domestic or familiar is considered safer than what is foreign and unfamiliar. In our story, domestic space and place are determined to be safer than foreign space and places and the people who inhabit them. But domestic space proves a dangerous and fatal place for 'Ênmishpat. No safe space exists for women where women are treated as sexual objects and as men's property.

"We" are your servants, the Levite says to the old man from Ephraim. The Levite permits the old man to have the same access to all his property that he enjoys. So the old man takes him in and by extension his property, including 'Ênmishpat. All the Levite needs is hospitality; he has food, wine, and servants; he describes his concubine as a maidservant ('mh) (19:19). "Maidservant" is a designation that gives the Levite's host greater access to 'Ênmishpat's body than if he had introduced her as his wife; he *dis*-members her and by doing so gives others permission to *dis*-respect or *dis*-member her, too. The old man provides hospitality—a safe place to eat, drink, and sleep; the old Ephraimite man and the Levite from Ephraim wash their feet, share a meal, and drink wine together. "Though the master is safe in the house, the woman is not."[55] Just as in the father-in-law's home, hospitality occurs among men. "He" and not "they" are welcomed into the old man's house (19:21). The hospitality between the men is literally described as men "being good to their heart" (19:22). When men's needs matter more than that of women and women are excluded as recipients of hospitality, women are *dis*-membered.

Dis-membering: Sacrificing Women to Protect Patriarchy and Masculinity

Eating and drinking among the two Israelite men is interrupted by perverse men of the city (later described as "brothers" and "lords of Gibeah") who want to know, sexually, the old man's male guest. The men pounding at the door refer to the old man as "the master [*ba'al*] of

---

55. Ibid., 72.

the house" (19:22; the Levite is ʾadonî, 19:26, 27). The old man chooses to sacrifice his virgin daughter and the Levite's lesser wife, ʾÊnmish-pat, rather than to allow the men to have sexual relations with his male guest. The men who have an appetite for men are offered a vir-gin daughter and a Levite's secondary wife; two women as surrogate for one man (19:24). Remember Lot's daughters (Gen 19:8)! An accept-able substitute for sexually ravishing one man is the offering up of two women (a lesser wife and a virgin daughter) as the objects of sexual vio-lence. They can be trafficked, subjected to gang rape, for the price of male masculinity. It is considered a "vile thing" to ravish a man. So the Levite sacrificed ʾÊnmishpat to save himself and the old man (19:25).

The "brothers" refuse the old man's compromise. But the Levite shoves ʾÊnmishpat out into the dark into the hands of the (Israelite) men. Secondary wives are more dispensable than virgins; they can more readily be subjected to sexual violence. The Levite casts ʾÊnmish-pat to the perverted and lust-driven "brothers," allowing them to do to her as is right in their own eyes just as he himself has done what was right in his own eyes. Patriarchal societies teach that it is the right of men to have access to women' bodies to satisfy their desires; that their rage is justified when what they've been taught they are entitled to is not given to them freely. Rape is an act of hostility and violence and not a crime of passion, even and especially when men (and women) rape their wives or traffic or expose their wives and daughters to oth-ers in order to protect their own bodies and "manhood." "She was a dispensable commodity, used to solve an annoyance between males."[56] Throughout the night, the "brothers" gang raped ʾÊnmishpat.

Black women are often most vulnerable and often "assaulted as an extension of antagonisms between men."[57] ʾÊnmishpat is assaulted as an extension of and as a substitute or surrogate for antagonisms between men and/or as a substitute or surrogate for male desire. The rapists do not reject the sacrifice of ʾÊnmishpat. Recently, the students in my "Engaging Texts and Contexts" course loudly expressed their shock and disbelief when we read the part of the story about the men wanting other men. When we read about the woman's brutal gang rape, however, no one made a sound!

In the morning when the men release ʾÊnmishpat (vv. 25–26), she has been so brutalized that she is unconscious. Where there are no

---

56. Yani Yoo, "Han-Laden Women: Korean 'Comfort Women' and Women in Judges 19–21," *Semeia* 78 (1997): 42.
57. Richie, *Arrested Justice*, 38.

laws or policies protecting women and children and the poor in patriarchal societies, men can do what they want to them and do so with impunity. Before the late twentieth century, white men and some black men could rape black women without being charged, indicted, and/or imprisoned. But black men could easily with little or no evidence be sentenced to death or life for allegedly raping white women.[58] Richie writes that black women experience direct sexual assaults but also "a disproportionate number of unwanted comments, uninvited physical advances, and undesired exposure to pornography at an alarming rate in their communities . . . [they] are assaulted in more brutal and degrading ways than other women. Weapons or objects are more often used, so Black women's injuries are worse than those of other groups of women. Black women are more likely to be raped repeatedly and to experience assaults that involve multiple perpetrators."[59]

'Ênmishpat manages to drag her emaciated body to the threshold of the door, where the men on the other side slept in *shalom* through the night of her terror. Julie Parker argues that placing her hand at the threshold and possibly attempting to enter the private domain of the house, traditionally associated with women's place/space, constitutes "a final act of self-determination in a futile attempt to find help or safety," and demonstrates her struggle to remain alive.[60]

The men who raped her saw no need to lose sleep over her victimization, and they did not. "They were most likely fast asleep in a drunken stupor after making their hearts merry."[61] In the light of day, the Levite gets up (*qŭm*), and he speaks to 'Ênmishpat without tenderness. She is not able to answer because she is either dead (the LXX) or she is simply too emaciated to respond. But he is not in the least dissuaded from continuing the journey on which he started. The young woman's terror in the night will not interfere with the Levite's business in the day.

Perhaps 'Ênmishpat's silence all along, even as she is "thrown to the wolves," is also a metaphor for how women are socialized to believe that they must sacrifice their own health, bodies, voices, happiness, and desires for the well-being of the men they marry, the men in their families, and the larger patriarchal community. Black women have been caught up in the loyalty trap, whereby they are to sacrifice their well-being for the sake of black men who are seen as more disadvan-

58. See Danielle L. McGuire, *At the Dark End of the Street: Black Women, Rape, and Resistance—A New History of the Civil Rights Movement from Rosa Parks to the Rise of Black Power* (New York: Vintage, 2011).
59. Richie, *Arrested Justice*, 45, 43.
60. Parker, "Re-membering the Dismembered," 177.
61. Reis, "The Levite's Concubine," 142.

taged than black women. Like Reagan's trickle-down economics, black women are to experience advancement as it trickles down through black men; they bear the burden and are accused when black men do not do well in society. Black women have been expected to bear a disproportionate burden for racial uplift and for caring for the community as a whole; the emotional manipulation of black women is contributed to by contemporary media—in novels, movies, and music videos. Because of the systemic biases and hindrances to economic advancement that black men endure, black women are expected to sacrifice their claims and access to resources and power. Black women continue to be blamed for the problems of the black community, including those that derive from lack of "power and subsequent victimization."[62] Richie argues that

> [i]t is important to return to the notion of "the trap of loyalty." The rhetoric of racial solidarity that can be used to manipulate Black women's commitment to individuals, their families, their peer groups to fully understand the harm created by social isolation and hostility. . . . Black women's roles in their communities have been organized around notions of allegiance to family, dedication to collective advancement, and respectability. This literature describes the sense that Black women are uniquely responsible for "racial uplift" because of their particular positioning in relationship to Black men and the larger social world.[63]

Dis-membering Her Memory: The Final Act of Injustice

The final stage of dis-membering occurs when the Levite cuts up his concubine's sexually abused body into twelve pieces and has them transported, by messengers, throughout the land of Israel (19:29-30). It is meant to protect patriarchy, a man's right to mutilate his own dis-membered property. Accompanying the Levite's mutilated cargo that he sent to his fellow Israelites is a message—a retelling of the story of his secondary wife's death from his perspective. It, of course, varies from the story the narrator relates. In his retelling, the Levite does not admit to being the initial object of male sexual desire. He does not portray himself as in any way complicit. The note addressed to the Israelites reads: "Has such a thing ever happened since the day that the Israelites came up from the land of Egypt until this day? Consider it, take counsel, and speak out" (19:30). It is not clear whether the

---

62. Richie, Arrested Justice, 46–47.
63. Ibid., 44.

brutal gang rape itself is considered heinous or if the real problem is the ultimate loss of the Levite's property. In any event, the objectification and cruel treatment of 'Ênmishpat as usable and disposable property is not unambiguously condemned. Is the Levite upset because they deprived him of the right to do with his own property as he wished, robbing him of having access to her body and her labor for as long as it pleased him? The rapists upset the patriarchal equilibrium. Julie Parker argues that the Levite is attempting to restore stability as a result of an atrocity: "These stories of [Concubine, Jezebel, and Anat] dismemberment prompt unification against a foe or obliteration of an enemy. The cultures that promulgated these texts affirm patriarchal values of domination and subjugation, usually with male characters as the decisive victors. While male gods are restored after being cut to pieces, the female humans become garbage."[64] In a patriarchal society a man has control of his own property and the right to destroy it himself will not be relinquished to his brothers in the streets. There are intragroup, tribal rules that protect a man's property rights, especially within the private domain of domestic space.

The Levite cannot tell the whole tale; he cannot bring himself to speak the words that tell the tale of men wanting men; but he has no problem repeating the brutality of the crime against 'Ênmishpat. All sexual violence should be offensive and shocking. Just because a society allows men free access to the bodies of women, young girls, and boys does not make it humane, nonoppressive, or less violent.

The Levite showed no compassion or grief over her death but, rather, anger at the impact of her death on his life and not any remembrance of her pain and death. She didn't even merit a proper burial. Her husband permitted her rape; he is complicit in it; he exposed her, pushed her out into the street in order to avoid being raped himself. If we start with the dismemberment by the Levite and not how we arrived at point in the narrative, we miss her full victimization—when society began to *dis*-member her. The Levite's mutilation of 'Ênmishpat's body erased, hid the full effect of what was done to her before the rape and including the rape. The mutilation and death, the final stage in 'Ênmishpat's *dis*-membering displays only parts of her body, dehumanizing her, making it almost impossible to re-member or view her as more than his damaged goods.

Just as the interrelatedness of the parties does not prevent the sex-

---

64. Parker, "Re-membering the Dismembered," 189.

ual exploitation and violence against the young woman, neither does it prevent the escalation of violence among brothers—the near extinction of an entire tribe because of the gang rape and murder of a Levite's lesser wife by members of that tribe. When Israel wages war against their brothers the Benjaminites, they defend the men who are both kinfolk and perpetrators of sexual violence and murder (20:13). A whole people (the Benjaminites) defend the right of a few men to do as they please. Maybe because if a few men cannot do as they please with one wife, surely the rest of them will not be able to do as they please when it comes to their women and the strangers among them (cf. Esth 1:1–21). The remnant of males who survive the massacre is presented with enslaved virginal women to have sexually, as they please, so as to guarantee their continued presence among the tribes.

In this story of 'Ênmishpat's *dis*-membering, mutilation, and death, the Levite is judge and jury. There is no investigation into her death or his complicity. In contemporary America, "Black women with lower social status are more likely to be victimized and their cases less rigorously investigated than their white counterparts."[65] Their lives, like 'Ênmishpat's, have been subjected to society's *dis*-membering and, too often, culminating in no justice and an early death.

Conclusion

I have attempted to read the story of the Levite's secondary wife through the lens of poor African American women's experience (and that of other poor people and people of color) of sexual violence, human trafficking, and incarceration. The complete mutilation and destruction of the lives of the most vulnerable among us begins with a *dis*-membering or a disrespect for them and their rights as human beings and full members of the society. Characteristic of this process of *dis*-membering is the denial, on the basis of race/ethnicity, class, gender, and sexuality, of basic human rights, access to needed resources, an equitable human wage, unbiased community policing, and protections afforded to the elite members of the dominant culture. Such *dis*-membering subjects the most vulnerable among us to more violence and eventually mutilation and annihilation. As Yani Yoo asserts, "the story invites the reader to witness and denounce the human evil against fellow human beings,"[66] especially marginalized women, chil-

65. Richie, *Arrested Justice*, 38.
66. Yani Yoo, "Han-Laden Women," 38.

dren, and their communities. 'Ênmishpat's abuse began with her *dis*-membering—her subordination and (mis)treatment predicated upon her intersectional identity—and eventually leading to her brutal gang rape and mutilation and culminating in her physical death and dismemberment. As people of God we bear the responsibility to work toward the creation of societies and a world in which all human beings experience the hospitality of God from cradle to the grave, characterized by equity and quality of life, regardless of gender, race/ethnicity, sexuality, age, or dis/ability. We must expose and resist all forms of oppression and violence.

Bibliography

Alexander, Michelle. *The New Jim Crow: Incarceration in an Age of Color Blindness.* New York: New Press, 2012.

Anderson, Cheryl B. "Reflections in an Interethnic/Racial Era on Interethnic/Racial Marriage in Ezra." In Randall C. Bailey, Tat-Siong Benny Liew, and Fernando F. Segovia, editors, *They Were All Together in One Place? Toward Minority Biblical Criticism*, 47–64. Semeia Studies 57. Atlanta: SBL Press, 2009.

Augustine of Hippo, St. *The Works of St. Augustine*, Sermon XLIII: 1–3, 15. *Nicene and Post-Nicene Fathers*, vol. 6: *Augustine: Sermon on the Mount, Harmony of the Gospels, Homilies on the Gospels.* Edited by Philip Schaff. Peabody, MA: Hendrickson, 2004.

Aymer, Margaret. *First Pure, then Peaceable: Frederick Douglass Reads James.* New York: T&T Clark, 2008.

_____. "Outrageous, Audacious, Courageous, Willful: Reading the Enslaved Girl of Acts 12." In Gay L. Byron and Vanessa Lovelace, editors, *Expanding the Discourse of Womanist Hermeneutics*, 265–90. Semeia Studies 85. Atlanta: SBL Press, 2016.

Bailey, Randall C. "Academic Biblical Interpretation among African Americans in the United States" In Vincent L. Wimbush, editor, *African Americans and the Bible: Sacred Texts and Social Textures*, 696–711. New York/London: Continuum, 2003.

_____. "Beyond Identification: The Use of Africans in Old Testament Poetry and Narratives." In Cain Hope Felder, editor, *Stony the Road We Trod: African American Biblical Interpretation*, 165–84. Minneapolis: Fortress Press, 1991.

_____. "The Cushite in David's Army Meets Ebedmelek: The Impact of Supremacist Ideologies on the Interpretations and Translations of Texts." In Randall C. Bailey, *Samuel Read through Different Eyes: The Collected Writings of Randall C. Bailey.* Grand Rapids: Eerdmans, forthcoming.

_____. "He Didn't Even Tell Us the Worst of It!" *Union Seminary Quarterly Review* 59, no. 1 (2005): 15–27.

_____. "'Is That Any Name for a Nice Hebrew Boy?' Exodus 2:1-10: The De-Africanization of an Israelite Hero." In Randall C. Bailey and Jacquelyn Grant, editors, *The Recovery of Black Presence: An Interdisciplinary Exploration*, 25–36. Nashville: Abingdon, 1995.

_____. *Samuel Read through Different Eyes: The Collected Writings of Randall C. Bailey*. Grand Rapids: Eerdmans, forthcoming.

_____. "'That's Why They Didn't Call the Book Hadassah!': The Interse(ct)/(x)ionality of Race/Ethnicity, Gender, and Sexuality in the book of Esther." In Randall C. Bailey, Tat-Siong Benny Liew, and Fernando F. Segovia, editors, *They Were All Together in One Place? Toward Minority Biblical Criticism*, 227–50. Semeia Studies 57. Atlanta: SBL Press, 2009.

_____, and Jacquelyn Grant, editors. *The Recovery of Black Presence: An Interdisciplinary Exploration*. Nashville: Abingdon, 1995.

_____. "'They Shall Become as White as Snow': When Bad Is Turned into Good." *Semeia* 76 (1996): 99–113.

_____, Tat-Siong Benny Liew, and Fernando F. Segovia, editors. *They Were All Together in One Place? Toward Minority Biblical Criticism*. Semeia Studies 57. Atlanta: SBL Press, 2009.

Bal, Mieke. *Death and Dissymmetry: The Politics of Coherence in the Book of Judges*. Chicago: University of Chicago Press, 1988.

Bales, Kevin, and Ron Soodalter. *The Slave Next Door: Human Trafficking and Slavery in America Today*. Berkeley: University of California Press, 2010.

Batstone, David. *Not for Sale: The Return of the Global Slave Trade—and How We Can Fight It*. New York: HarperCollins, 2007.

Bell, Jamaal. "Race and Human Trafficking in U.S.: Unclear but Undeniable." The Huffington Post. May 25, 2011. http://www.huffingtonpost.com/jamaal-bell/race-and-human-traffickin_b_569795.html.

Bhabha, Homi K. "The Other Question: Stereotype, Discrimination and the Discourse of Colonialism." In Homi K. Bhabha, editor, *The Location of Culture*, 94–120. New York: Routledge, 1994.

Bibb, Henry. "Narrative of the Life and Adventures of Henry Bibb, an American Slave, Written by Himself . . . (1849)" In William L. Andrews and Henry Louis Gates Jr., editors, *Slave Narratives*, 425–566. New York: Library of America, 2000.

Black, Max. *Metaphors: Studies in Language and Philosophy*. Ithaca: Cornell University Press, 1962.

Blount, Brian K. *Can I Get a Witness? Reading Revelation through African American Culture*. Louisville: Westminster John Knox, 2005.

_____. *Cultural Interpretation: Reorienting New Testament Criticism.* Minneapolis: Fortress Press, 1995.

_____. *Go Preach! Mark's Kingdom Message and the Black Church Today.* Maryknoll, NY: Orbis, 1998.

_____. "A Socio-Rhetorical Analysis of Simon of Cyrene." *Semeia* 63 (1993): 171–98.

_____. *Then the Whisper Put on Flesh: New Testament Ethics in an African American Context.* Nashville: Abingdon, 2001.

_____, general editor. With Cain Hope Felder, Clarice J. Martin, and Emerson B. Powery, associate editors. *True to Our Native Land: An African American Commentary of the New Testament.* Minneapolis: Fortress Press, 2007.

Boring, M. Eugene. "Matthew." In Leander Keck, editor, *The New Interpreters Bible,* vol. 8: *General Articles on the New Testament, Matthew, Mark,* 87–506. Nashville: Abingdon, 1995.

Braxton, Brad Ronnell. *No Longer Slaves: Galatians and African American Experience.* Collegeville, MN: Liturgical, 2002.

Bridgeman, Valerie. "Jonah." In Hugh R. Page Jr., general editor, *The Africana Bible: Reading Israel's Scriptures from Africa and the African Diaspora,* 183–88. Minneapolis: Fortress Press, 2010.

Brown, Michael Joseph. *Blackening the Bible: The Aims of African American Biblical Scholarship.* Harrisburg, PA: Trinity, 2004.

Burgh, Theodore W. "Black Biblical Interpretation and Near Eastern Archaeology." *Black Theology* 4, no. 2 (2006): 138–50.

Byron, Gay L. "Ancient Ethiopia and the New Testament: Ethnic (Con)texts and Racialized (Sub)texts." In Randall C. Bailey, Tat-Siong Benny Liew, and Fernando F. Segovia, editors, *They Were All Together in One Place? Toward Minority Biblical Criticism,* 161–90. Semeia Studies 57. Atlanta: SBL Press, 2009.

_____. "Black Collectors and Keepers of Tradition: Resources for a Womanist Biblical Ethic of (Re)Interpretation." In Gay L. Byron and Vanessa Lovelace, editors, *Expanding the Discourse of Womanist Hermeneutics,* 187–208. Semeia Studies 85. Atlanta: SBL Press, 2016.

_____, and Vanessa Lovelace, editors. *Expanding the Discourse of Womanist Hermeneutics.* Semeia Studies 85. Atlanta: SBL Press, 2016.

_____. *Symbolic Blackness and Ethnic Difference in Early Christian Literature: Blackened by the Skins.* New York: Routledge, 2002.

Byron, Tammy K. "'A Catechism for Their Special Use': Slave Catechisms in the Antebellum South." PhD dissertation, University of Arkansas, 2008.

Callahan, Allen Dwight. *The Talking Book: African Americans and the Bible.* New Haven: Yale University Press, 2006.

Cannon, Katie Geneva. *Katie's Canon: Womanism and the Soul of the Black Community*. New York: Bloomsbury, 1998.

Carter, Warren. "The Gospel of Matthew." In Fernando F. Segovia and R. S. Sugirtharajh, editors, *A Postcolonial Commentary of the New Testament Writings*, 69–103. New York: T&T Clark, 2009.

_____. *Matthew and the Margins: A Socio-Political and Religious Reading*. Sheffield, UK: Sheffield University Press, 2000.

Clark, Septima Poinsette. *Echo in My Soul*. New York: E. P. Dutton, 1962.

Collins, Patricia Hill, and Sirma Bilge. *Intersectionality*. Malden, MA: Polity, 2016.

Cone, James H. *Black Theology and Black Power*. New York: Harper & Row, 1969.

_____. *God of the Oppressed*. Maryknoll, NY: Orbis, 1997.

Copher, Charles B. *Black Biblical Studies: An Anthology of Charles B. Copher*. Chicago: Black Light Fellowship, 1993.

_____. "The Bible and the African Experience: The Biblical Period." *Journal of the Interdenominational Theological Center* 13 (1988): 57–79.

_____. "The Black Presence in the Old Testament." In Cain Hope Felder, editor, *Stony the Road We Trod: African American Biblical Interpretation*, 147–49. Minneapolis: Fortress Press, 1991.

Crowder, Stephanie Buckhanon. "The New Testament of R&B." In Thomas B. Slater, editor, *Afrocentric Interpretations of Jesus and the Gospel Tradition: Things Black Scholars See That White Scholars Overlook*, 19–36. Lewiston, NY: Edwin Mellen, 2015.

_____. *When Momma Speaks: The Bible and Motherhood from a Womanist Perspective*. Louisville: Westminster John Knox, 2016.

Darden, Lynne St. Clair. *Scripturalizing Revelation: An African American Postcolonial Reading of Empire*. Atlanta: SBL Press, 2015.

Davis, Stacy. "Susanna." In Hugh R. Page Jr., general editor, *The Africana Bible: Reading Israel's Scriptures from Africa and the African Diaspora*, 293–95. Minneapolis: Fortress Press, 2010.

Delgado, Richard, and Jean Stefancic. *Critical Race Theory. An Introduction,* Second Edition. New York and London: New York University Press, 2012.

Deutsch, Celia. "Wisdom in Matthew: Transformation of a Symbol." *Novum Testamentum* 32 (1990): 13–47.

Doezema, Jo. "Who Gets to Choose? Coercion, Consent and the UN Trafficking Protocol." *Gender and Development* 10 (2002): 20–27.

Douglas, Kelly Brown. *Sexuality and the Black Church: A Womanist Perspective*. Maryknoll, NY: Orbis, 1999.

_____. *Stand Your Ground: Black Bodies and the Justice of God*. Maryknoll, NY: Orbis, 2015.

Douglass, Frederick. *My Bondage and My Freedom.* 1855 Edition. New York: Dover Publications, 1969.

_____. *Narrative of the Life of Frederick Douglass, an American Slave, Written by Himself* (Boston, 1845). In William L. Andrews and Henry Louis Gates Jr., editors, *Slave Narratives,* 267–368. New York: Library of America, 2000.

Dube, Musa. *Postcolonial Feminist Interpretation of the Bible.* St. Louis: Chalice, 2000.

DuBois, Page. *Torture and Truth: The New Ancient World.* New York/London: Routledge, 1991.

Du Bois, W. E. B. *The Souls of Black Folk.* In *W. E .B. Du Bois: Writings,* 357–547. Edited by Nathan Huggins. New York: Library of America, 1987.

Equiano, Olaudah. "Interesting Narrative of the Life of Olaudah Equiano, or Gustavo Vassa, the African. Written by Himself (1789)." In William L. Andrews and Henry Louis Gates Jr., editors, *Slave Narratives,* 49–242. New York: Library of America, 2000.

Everitt, Anthony. *Cicero: The Life and Times of Rome's Greatest Politician.* New York: Random House, 2003.

Exum, Cheryl J. *Fragmented Women: Feminist (Sub)versions of Biblical Narratives.* Journal for the Study of the Old Testament Supplement Series 163. Sheffield, UK: Sheffield University Press, 1993.

Felder, Cain Hope, editor. *Holy Bible: African American Jubilee Edition.* Contemporary English Version. New York: American Bible Society, 1999.

_____, editor. *The Original African Heritage Study Bible.* King James Version. Iowa Falls, IA: World Bible Publishers, 1993.

_____. "Race, Racism, and the Biblical Narratives." In Cain Hope Felder, editor, *Stony the Road We Trod: African American Biblical Interpretation,* 129–35. Minneapolis: Fortress Press, 1991.

_____, editor. *Stony the Road We Trod: African American Biblical Interpretation.* Minneapolis: Fortress Press, 1991.

_____. *Troubling Biblical Waters: Race, Class and Family.* Maryknoll, NY: Orbis, 1989.

Fiorenza, Elisabeth Schüssler. *Jesus: Miriam's Child, Sophia's Prophet: Critical Issues in Feminist Christology.* New York: Continuum, 1995.

Foskett, Mary F. *A Virgin Conceived: Mary and Classical Representations of Virginity.* Bloomington: Indiana University Press, 2002.

Freire, Paulo. *The Pedagogy of the Oppressed.* New York: Continuum, 1997.

Frostenson, Sarah. "Most Terrorists Attacks in the US are Committed by Americans—Not Foreigners." Vox. September 9, 2016. http://www.vox.com/2015/11/23/9765718/domestic-terrorism-threat.

Gafney, Wil. "Reading the Hebrew Bible Responsibly." In Hugh R. Page Jr., general editor, *The Africana Bible: Reading Israel's Scriptures from Africa and the African Diaspora*, 45–54. Minneapolis: Fortress Press, 2010.

_____. "What Judges 19 Has to Say About Domestic Violence." *Sojourners*. October 5, 2015. https://sojo.net/print/217296.

_____. *Womanist Midrash: A Reintroduction to the Women of the Torah and the Throne*. Louisville: Westminster John Knox, 2017.

_____. "A Womanist Midrash of Zipporah." In Mitzi J. Smith, editor, *I Found God in Me: A Womanist Biblical Hermeneutics Reader*, 131–57. Eugene, OR: Cascade, 2015.

Garnsey, Peter. *Ideas of Slavery from Aristotle to Augustine*. Cambridge: Cambridge University Press, 1996.

Glancy, Jennifer A. *Slavery in the Early Church*. Minneapolis: Fortress Press, 2006.

Gorman, Michael. *Elements of Biblical Exegesis: A Basic Guide for Students and Ministers*. Peabody, MA: Hendrickson, 2005.

Gosse, Dave. "Examining the Promulgation and Impact of the Great Commission in the Caribbean, 1942–1970: A Historical Analysis." In Mitzi J. Smith, and Lalitha Jayachitra, editors, *Teaching All Nations: Interrogating the Matthean Great Commission*, 33–56. Minneapolis: Fortress Press, 2014.

Grant, Jacquelyn. *White Woman's Christ and Black Women's Jesus: Feminist Christology and Womanist Response*. Atlanta: Scholars, 1989.

Green, Bridgette. "'Nobody's Free until Everybody's Free': Exploring Gender and Class Injustice in a Story about Children (Luke 18:15-17)." In Gay L. Byron and Vanessa Lovelace, editors, *Expanding the Discourse of Womanist Hermeneutics*, 291–310. Semeia Studies 85. Atlanta: SBL Press, 2016.

Gronniosaw, James Albert Ukawsaw. "A Narrative of the Most Remarkable Particulars in the Life of James Albert Ukawsaw Gronniosaw, an African Prince, As related by Himself (1772)." In William L. Andrews and Henry Louis Gates Jr., editors, *Slave Narratives*, 1–34. New York: Library of America, 2000.

Guerra, Maria. "Fact Sheet: The State of African American Women in the United States." Center for American Progress. November 7, 2013. https://www.americanprogress.org/issues/race/report/2013/11/07/79165/fact-sheet-the-state-of-african-american-women-in-the-united-states.

Hamer, Fannie Lou. "It's in Your Hands." In Gerda Lerner, editor, *Black Women in White America: A Documentary History*, 609–14. New York: Vintage, 1972.

Hancock, Ange-Marie. *The Politics of Disgust*. New York: New York University Press, 2004.

Harrill, J. Albert. "The Psychology of Slaves in the Gospel Parables. A Case Study in Social History." *Biblische Zeitschrift* 55 (2011): 63–74.

Harris, Fredrick, and Robert Lieberman. *Beyond Discrimination: Racial Inequality in a Postracist Era*. New York: Russell Sage Foundation, 2013.

Haugen, Gary A. *The Locus Effect. Why the End of Poverty Requires the End of Violence*. New York and London: Oxford University Press, 2015.

Hendricks, Obery. "Guerrilla Exegesis: A Post-Modern Proposal for Insurgent African American Biblical Interpretation." *Journal of the Interdenominational Theological Center* 22 (1994): 92–109.

Hippolytus of Rome. "Appendix to His Works. Containing Dubious and Spurious Pieces," XLII, 53. *Ante-Nicene Fathers, Appendix*, vol. 5. Edited by Alexander Roberts and James Donaldson. Peabody, MA: Hendrickson, 1995.

Hoyt, Thomas, Jr. "Biblical Interpreters and Black Theology." In Gayraud S. Wilmore and James H. Cone, editors, *Black Theology: A Documentary History, vol. 2: 1980-1992*, 196–209. Maryknoll, NY: Orbis, 1996.

Jones-Warsaw, Koala. "Toward a Womanist Hermeneutic: A Reading of Judges 19-21." In Athalya Brenner, editor, *A Feminist Companion to Judges*, 172–86. Sheffield, UK: Sheffield University Press, 1993.

Junior, Nyasha. *An Introduction to Womanist Biblical Interpretation*. Louisville: Westminster John Knox, 2015.

Kelly, Liz. "The Wrong Debate: Reflections on Why Force Is Not the Key Issue with Respect to Trafficking in Women for Sexual Exploitation." *Feminist Review* 73 (2003): 139–44.

Kempadoo, Kamala, and Jo Doezema, editors. *Global Sex Workers: Rights, Resistance and Redefinition*. New York/London: Routledge, 1998.

Levine, Amy-Jill. "Gospel of Matthew." In Carol A. Newsom, Sharon H. Ringe, and Jacqueline E. Lapsley, editors, *The Women's Bible Commentary: Twentieth-Anniversary Edition, Revised and Updated*, 465–77. Louisville: Westminster John Knox, 2012.

Lewis, Lloyd. "An African American Appraisal of the Philemon–Paul–Onesimus Triangle." In Cain Hope Felder, editor, *Stony the Road We Trod: African American Biblical Interpretation*, 232–46. Minneapolis: Fortress Press, 1991.

Lorde, Audre. *Sister Outsider*. Freedom, CA: Crossing, 1984.

Marbury, Herbert Robinson. *Pillars of Cloud and Fire: The Politics of Exodus in African American Biblical Interpretation*. New York: New York University Press, 2015.

Martin, Clarice J. "A Chamberlain's Journey and the Challenge of Interpretation for Liberation." *Semeia* 47 (1989): 105–35.

_____. "The Function of Acts 8:26-40 within the Narrative Structure of the Book of Acts: The Significance of the Eunuch's Provenance for Acts 1:8c." PhD dissertation, Duke University, 1985.

_____. "The *Haustafeln* (Household Codes) in African American Biblical Interpretation: 'Free Slaves' and 'Subordinate Women.'" In Cain Hope Felder,

Stony the Road We Trod: African American Biblical Interpretation, 206–231. Minneapolis: Fortress Press, 1991.

_____. "Polishing the Unclouded Mirror: A Womanist Reading of Revelation 18:13." In David Rhoads, ed., *From Every People and Nation: The Book of Revelation in Intercultural Perspective*, 82–109. Minneapolis: Fortress Press, 2005.

_____. "Womanist Interpretations of the New Testament: The Quest for Holistic and Inclusive Translation and Interpretation." *Journal of Feminist Studies in Religion* 6, no. 2 (1990): 41–61.

McClenney-Sadler, Madeline. "Cry Witch: The Embers Still Burn." In Cheryl A. Kirk-Duggan, editor, *Pregnant Passion, Gender, Sex, and Violence in the Bible*, 116–41. Semeia Studies 44. Atlanta: SBL Press, 2003.

McGuire, Danielle L. *At the Dark End of the Street: Black Women, Rape, and Resistance—A New History of the Civil Rights Movement from Rosa Parks to the Rise of Black Power*. New York: Vintage, 2011.

Methodius. *Banquet of the Ten Virgins*, "The Parable of the Virgins." Discourse VI, Chapter III, 330; Discourse VII, Chapter I.

Myers, William H. *God's Yes Was Louder than My No. Rethinking the African American Call to Ministry*. Grand Rapids: Eerdmans/Trenton, NY: African Word, 1994.

_____. "The Hermeneutical Dilemma of the African American Biblical Student." In Cain Hope Felder, editor, *Stony the Road We Trod: African American Biblical Interpretation*, 40–56. Minneapolis: Fortress Press, 1991.

_____. *The Irresistible Urge to Preach: A Collection of African American Call Stories*. Atlanta: Aaron, 1992.

Neely, Cheryl L. *You're Dead—So What? Media, Policy, and the Invisibility of Black Women as Victims of Homicide*. East Lansing: Michigan State University Press, 2015.

Nijmegen, Erik Eynikel. "Judges 19–21, An 'Appendix': Rape, Murder, War and Abduction," *Communio Viatorum* 47, no. 2 (2005): 101–15.

Norton, Yolanda. "Silenced Struggles for Survival: Finding Life in Death in the Book of Ruth." In Mitzi J. Smith, editor, *I Found God in Me: A Womanist Biblical Hermeneutics Reader*, 265–79. Eugene, OR: Cascade, 2015.

Oakes, Penelope J., S. Alexander Haslam, Brenda Morrison, and Diana Grace. "Becoming an In-Group: Reexamining the Impact of Familiarity on Perceptions of Group Homogeneity." *Social Psychology Quarterly* 58, no. 1 (1995): 52–60.

Okyere-Manu, Beatrice. "Colonial Mission and the Great Commission in Africa." In Mitzi J. Smith, and Lalitha Jayachitra, editors, *Teaching All Nations: Interrogating the Matthean Great Commission*, 15–32. Minneapolis: Fortress Press, 2014.

Page, Hugh R., Jr., general editor. *The Africana Bible: Reading Israel's Scriptures from Africa and the African Diaspora*. Minneapolis: Fortress Press, 2010.

_____. *Israel's Poetry of Resistance*. Minneapolis: Fortress Press, 2013.

Palmer, B. M. *A Plain and Easy Catechism, Designed Chiefly for the Benefit of Coloured Persons, to Which Are Annexed Suitable Prayers and Hymns*. Charleston, SC: Observer Office Press, 1828.

Parker, Julie Faith. "Re-membering the Dismembered: Piecing Together Meaning from Stories of Women and Body Parts in Ancient Near Eastern Literature." *Biblical Interpretation* 23 (2015): 174–90.

Patterson, Orlando. *Slavery and Social Death: A Comparative Study*. Cambridge, MA: Harvard University Press, 1982.

Piecora, Christina. "Female Inmates and Sexual Assault." *Jurist*. Student Commentary. September 14, 2014. http://www.jurist.org/dateline/2014/09/christina-piecora-female-inmates.php.

Plutarch. "Life of Romulus." In Bernadotte Perrin, translator, *Parallel Lives*, 29–31. Loeb Classical Library 1. Cambridge, MA: Harvard University Press, 1914.

Powery, Emerson B., and Rodney S. Sadler Jr. *The Genesis of Liberation: Biblical Interpretation in the Antebellum Narratives of the Enslaved*. Louisville: Westminster John Knox, 2016.

Reid, Stephen Breck. *Experience and Tradition: A Primer in Black Biblical Hermeneutics*. Nashville: Abingdon, 1990.

Reis, Pamela. "The Levite's Concubine: New Light on a Dark Story." *Scandinavian Journal of the Old Testament* 20, no. 1 (2006): 125–46.

Rice, Gene. "The African Roots of the Prophet Zephaniah." *Journal of Religious Thought* 36, no. 1 (Spring-Summer 1979): 21–31.

_____. "The Curse That Never Was (Genesis 9:18-27)." *Journal of Religious Thought* 29 (1972): 5–27.

Richie, Beth E. *Arrested Justice: Black Women, Violence, and America's Prison Nation*. New York: New York University Press, 2012.

Riggs, Marcia Y. *Can I Get a Witness? Prophetic Religious Voices of African American Women: An Anthology*. Maryknoll, NY: Orbis, 1997.

Rodger, A. F. "Peculium." In S. Hornblower and A. Spawforth, eds., *The Oxford Classical Dictionary*, 110. Third edition. New York: Oxford University Press, 1996.

Rogers, Elice E. "Afritics from Margin to Center: Theorizing the Politics of African American Women as Political Leaders." *Journal of Black Studies* 35, no. 6 (2005): 701–14.

Ross, Rosetta. *Witnessing and Testifying: Black Women, Religion, and Civil Rights*. Minneapolis: Fortress Press, 2003.

Russaw, Kimberly. "Wisdom in the Garden: The Woman of Genesis 3 and Alice Walker's *Sophia*." In Mitzi J. Smith, editor, *I Found God in Me: A Womanist Biblical Hermeneutics Reader*, 222–34. Eugene, OR: Cascade, 2015.

Sadler, Rodney. *Can a Cushite Change His Skin? An Examination of Race, Ethnicity and Othering in the Hebrew Bible.* New York: Bloomsbury T&T Clark, 2009.

Said, Edward. *Culture and Imperialism.* New York: Vintage, 1994.

St. Clair, Raquel. *Call and Consequences: A Womanist Reading of the Gospel of Mark.* Minneapolis: Fortress Press, 2008.

Sanders, Boykin. "In Search of a Face for Simon the Cyrene." In Randall C. Bailey and Jacquelyn Grant, editors, *The Recovery of Black Presence: An Interdisciplinary Exploration*, 51–64. Nashville: Abingdon, 1995.

Schroeder, Joy A. "Dismembering the Adulteress: Sixteenth-Century Commentary on the Narrative of the Levite's Concubine (Judges 19–21)." *Seminary Ridge Review* 9, no. 2 (2007): 5–24.

Sechrest, Love. *A Former Jew: Paul and the Dialectics of Race.* New York: T&T Clark, 2010.

Segovia, Fernando F. "Introduction: Configurations, Approaches, Findings, Stances." In Fernando F. Segovia and R. S. Sugirtharajh, editors, *A Postcolonial Commentary of the New Testament Writings*, 1–68. New York: T&T Clark, 2009.

_____. "Postcolonial Criticism and the Gospel of Matthew." In Mark Allan Powell, editor, *Methods for Matthew*, 194–238. Cambridge: Cambridge University Press, 2009.

Seneca. *Ad Lucilum Epistulae Morales.* Translated by J. W. Basore. Loeb Classical Library 47. Cambridge, MA: Harvard University Press, 1979.

Shannon, David T. "'An Ante-bellum Sermon': A Resource for an African American Hermeneutic." In Cain Hope Felder, editor, *Stony the Road We Trod: African American Biblical Interpretation*, 98–125. Minneapolis: Fortress Press, 1991.

Sheriff, Natasja. "US cited for police violence, racism in scathing UN review on human rights." Aljazeera America. May 11, 2015. http://america.aljazeera.com/articles/2015/5/11/us-faces-scathing-un-review-on-human-rights-record.html.

Slater, Thomas B., editor. *Afrocentric Interpretations of Jesus and the Gospel Tradition: Things Black Scholars See That White Scholars Overlook.* Lewiston, NY: Edwin Mellen, 2015.

_____. "Howard Thurman: His Influence and His Relationship to the Third Quest." In Thomas B. Slater, editor, *Afrocentric Interpretations of Jesus and the Gospel Tradition: Things Black Scholars See That White Scholars Overlook*, 37–55. Lewiston, NY: Edwin Mellen, 2015.

Smith, Abraham. "'I Saw the Book Talk': A Cultural Studies Approach to the Ethics of an African American Biblical Hermeneutics." *Semeia* 77 (1997): 115–38.

_____. "Toni Morrison's Song of Solomon: the Blues and the Bible." In Randall Bailey and Jacquelyn Grant, editors, *Recovery of the Black Presence*, 107–15.

Smith, J. Z. "What a Difference a Difference Makes." In Jacob Neusner and Ernest S. Frerichs, editors, *"To See Ourselves as Others See Us": Christians, Jews, "Others" in Late Antiquity*, 3–48. Chico, CA: Scholars, 1985.

Smith, Mitzi J. "Give Me Jesus: Salvation History in the Spirituals." In Thomas B. Slater, editor, *Afrocentric Interpretations of Jesus and the Gospel Tradition: Things Black Scholars See That White Scholars Overlook*, 57–88. Lewiston, NY: Edwin Mellen, 2015.

_____. "God is a Black Woman and She is Divine." Womanistprof.blogspot.com. March 11, 2011. http://womanistntprof.blogspot.com/2011/03/god-is-black-woman-and-she-is-divine.html.

_____, editor. *I Found God in Me: A Womanist Biblical Hermeneutics Reader*. Eugene, OR: Cascade, 2015.

_____. "Race, Gender, and the Politics of 'Sass': Reading Mark 7:24-20 through a Womanist Lens of Intersectionality and Inter(con)textuality." In Gay L. Byron and Vanessa Lovelace, editors, *Expanding the Discourse of Womanist Hermeneutics*, 95–112. Semeia Studies 85. Atlanta: SBL Press, 2016.

_____. "Reading the Story of the Levite's Concubine through the Lens of Modern-Day Sex Trafficking." *Ashland Theological Journal* 41 (2009): 15–34.

_____. "Slavery in the Early Church." In Brian K. Blount, general editor, with Cain Hope Felder, Clarice J. Martin, and Emerson B. Powery, associate editors, *True to Our Native Land: An African American New Testament Commentary*, 11–22. Minneapolis: Fortress Press, 2007.

_____, and Lalitha Jayachitra, editors. *Teaching All Nations: Interrogating the Matthean Great Commission*. Minneapolis: Fortress, 2014.

_____. "'Unbossed and Unbought': Zilpha Elaw and Old Elizabeth and a Political Discourse of Origins." *Black Theology* 9, no. 3 (2011): 287–311.

_____. "U.S. Colonial Missions to African Slaves: Catechizing Black Souls, Traumatizing the Black *Psychē*." In Mitzi J. Smith and Lalitha Jayachitra, editors, *Teaching All Nations: Interrogating the Matthean Great Commission*, 57–88. Minneapolis: Fortress Press, 2014.

_____. *Womanist Sass and Talk Back: Intersectionality, Social (In)Justice, and Biblical Interpretation*. Eugene, OR: Cascade, 2017.

Smith, Shanell T. *The Woman Babylon and the Marks of Empire: Reading Revelation with a Postcolonial Womanist Hermeneutics of Ambiveilence.* Emerging Scholars. Minneapolis: Fortress Press, 2014.

Snowden, Frank M., Jr. *Blacks in Antiquity: Ethiopians in the Greco-Roman Experience.* Cambridge, MA: Harvard University Press, 1970.

Stetzer, Bill. "Biblical Illiteracy by the Numbers Part 1: The Challenge." *Christianity Today.* October 17, 2014. http://www.christianitytoday.com/edstetzer/2014/october/biblical-illiteracy-by-numbers.html.

_____. "The Epidemic of Biblical Illiteracy in Our Churches." *Christianity Today.* July 6, 2015. http://www.christianitytoday.com/edstetzer/2015/july/epidemic-of-bible-illiteracy-in-our-churches.html.

Stokes, Adam Oliver. "Bel and the Dragon." In Hugh R. Page Jr., general editor, *The Africana Bible: Reading Israel's Scriptures from Africa and the African Diaspora,* 314–15. Minneapolis: Fortress Press, 2010.

Stubbs, Monya. *Indebted Love: Paul's Subjection Language in Romans.* Eugene, OR: Wipf and Stock, 2013.

Tate, W. Randolph. *Biblical Interpretation: An Integrative Approach.* Peabody, MA: Hendrickson, 1997.

Terkel, Amanda. "GOP Congressman Insists White Terrorists Attacks are Totally Different," The Huffington Post. February 7, 2017. http://www.huffingtonpost.com/entry/sean-duffy-terrorism_us_589a081ce4b0c1284f28854c.

Terrell, JoAnne Marie. *Power in the Blood? The Cross in the African American Experience.* Eugene, OR: Wipf and Stock, 2005.

Thurman, Howard. *Jesus and the Disinherited.* Boston: Beacon, 1976.

Townes, Emilie M. *Womanist Ethics and the Cultural Production of Evil.* New York: Palgrave Macmillan, 2006.

Trible, Phyllis. *Texts of Terror: Literary-Feminist Readings of Biblical Narratives.* Overtures to Biblical Theology. Minneapolis: Fortress Press, 1984.

Turner, Nat. "The Confessions of Nat Turner, the Leader of the late Insurrections in Southampton, VA . . . (1831)." In William L. Andrews and Henry Louis Gates Jr., editors, *Slave Narratives,* 243–66. New York: Library of America, 2000.

Vickers, Steve. "Lost Jewish Tribe 'Found in Zimbabwe'." Harare: BBC News. March 8, 2010. http://newsvote.bbc.co.uk/mpapps/pagetools/print/news.bbc.co.uk/2/hi/africa/8550614.stm?ad=1 .

Walker, Alice. "Coming Apart." In Laura Lederer, editor, *Take Back the Night,* 84–93. New York: Bantam, 1979.

_____. *In Our Mothers' Gardens: Womanist Prose.* San Diego: Harcourt Brace, 1983.

Warrior, Robert. "Canaanites, Cowboys, and Indians: Canaanites, Cowboys and

Indians." In R. S. Sugirtharajah, editor, *Voices from the Margins: Interpreting the Bible in the Third World*, 287–95. London: SPCK, 1991.

Waters, John W. "Who Was Hagar?" In Cain Hope Felder, editor, *Stony the Road We Trod: African American Biblical Interpretation*, 187–205. Minneapolis: Fortress Press, 1991.

Weems, Renita J. "The Hebrew Women Are Not Like the Egyptian Women: The Ideology of Race, Gender and Sexual Reproduction in Exodus 1." *Semeia* 59 (1992): 25–34.

_____. *Just a Sister Away: A Womanist Vision of Women's Relationships in the Bible.* Philadelphia: Innisfree/San Diego: LuraMedia, 1988. Second edition: *Just a Sister Away: Understanding the Timeless Connection between Women of Today and Women in the Bible.* New York: Warner/West Bloomfield, MI: Walk Worthy, 2005.

_____. "Reading *Her Way* through the Struggle: African American Women and the Bible." In Cain Hope Felder, editor, *Stony the Road We Trod: African American Biblical Interpretation*, 57–79. Minneapolis: Fortress Press, 1991.

Wilder, Craig Steven. *Ebony and Ivy: Race, Slavery, and the Troubled History of America's Universities.* New York: Bloomsbury, 2014.

Williams, Delores S. *Sisters in the Wilderness: The Challenge of Womanist God-Talk.* Maryknoll, NY: Orbis, 1993.

Williams, Demetrius K. *An End to This Strife: The Politics of Gender in African American Churches.* Minneapolis: Fortress Press, 2004.

_____. "'Upon All Flesh': Acts 2, African Americans and Intersectional Realities." In Randall C. Bailey, Tat-Siong Benny Liew, and Fernando F. Segovia, editors, *They Were All Together in One Place? Toward Minority Biblical Criticism*, 289–310. Semeia Studies 57. Atlanta: SBL Press, 2009.

Wimbush, Vincent L. *African Americans and the Bible: Sacred Texts and Social Textures.* New York/London: Continuum, 2003.

_____. "The Bible and African Americans: An Outline of an Interpretative History." In Cain Hope Felder, editor, *Stony the Road We Trod: African American Biblical Interpretation*, 81–97. Minneapolis: Fortress Press, 1991.

_____, editor. *MisReading America: Scriptures and Difference.* New York: Oxford University Press, 2013.

_____. *Scripturalizing the Human: The Written as Political.* London/New York: Routledge, 2015.

_____. *White Men's Magic: Scripturalization as Slavery.* New York/London: Oxford University Press, 2012.

Winborne, Sheila F. "Images of Jesus in Advancing the Great Commission." In Mitzi J. Smith and Lalitha Jayachitra, editors, *Teaching All Nations: Interrogating the Matthean Great Commission*, 159–73. Minneapolis: Fortress Press, 2014.

Yoo, Yani. "Han-Laden Women: Korean 'Comfort Women' and Women in Judges 19–21." *Semeia* 78 (1997): 37–46.

Index